NOOK eReaders

FOR

DUMMIES®

PORTABLE EDITION

by Corey Sandler

WILEY

John Wiley & Sons, Inc.

NOOK® eReaders For Dummies® Portable Edition

Published by
John Wiley & Sons, Inc.
111 River Street
Hoboken, NJ 07030-5774

www.wiley.com

Copyright © 2013 by John Wiley & Sons, Inc., Hoboken, New Jersey

Published by John Wiley & Sons, Inc., Hoboken, New Jersey

Published simultaneously in Canada

For general information on our other products and services, please contact our Customer Care Department within the U.S. at 877-762-2974, outside the U.S. at 317-572-3993, or fax 317-572-4002.

For technical support, please visit www.wiley.com/techsupport.

Wiley publishes in a variety of print and electronic formats and by print-on-demand. Some material included with standard print versions of this book may not be included in e-books or in print-on-demand. If this book refers to media such as a CD or DVD that is not included in the version you purchased, you may download this material at http://booksupport.wiley.com. For more information about Wiley products, visit www.wiley.com.

Library of Congress Control Number: 2012949511

ISBN 978-1-118-44044-5 (pbk); ISBN 978-1-118-44043-8 (ebk); ISBN 978-1-118-44041-4 (ebk); ISBN 978-1-118-44042-1 (ebk)

Manufactured in the United States of America

10 9 8 7 6 5 4 3 2 1

WILEY

About the Author

Corey Sandler is a voracious reader and also an indefatigable author of books. Also magazines and, back in the days between Gutenberg and the arrival of the first eReader, newspapers.

He has written more than 200 books at last count, about computers, technology, history, sports, and business. Sandler travels all over the world conducting research and lecturing; he has zoomed past the century mark of countries visited: watch out Moldova, Kaliningrad, and Bolivia — you're up next.

Okay, so sometimes he is fatigable. That happens when you carry 150 pounds of luggage including a laptop, three cameras and lenses, a dozen books to read and consult, and a hogshead of lecture notes printed out and neatly bound to sit on a lectern. And that's why he's a fan of electronic books. They're good for his back.

Sandler studied journalism (and took some courses to program a gigantic mainframe computer) at Syracuse University. He began his career as a daily newspaper reporter in Ohio and then New York, moving on to a post as a correspondent for The Associated Press. From there he joined Ziff-Davis Publishing as the first executive editor of *PC Magazine*. He wrote his first book about computers in 1983 and hasn't come close to stopping.

When he's not on the road and living on his smartphone and computer, he's at home on Nantucket Island thirty miles out to sea off the coast of Massachusetts. He shares his life with his wife Janice; their two grown children have their own careers elsewhere on the continent.

You can see Sandler's current list of books on his website at www.sandlerbooks.com and send an e-mail through the links you find there. He promises to respond to courteous inquiries as quickly as he can. Spam, on the other hand, will be dumped into the Atlantic Ocean.

Dedication

This book, like all I've written, is dedicated to my family. They are the first to know when Dad has a new book to write: first the excitement, then the dread, then the weeks of silent solitude interspersed with the occasional screams of "Eureka!" and finally the thrill of victory — or at least satisfaction — when the electronic file leaves my computer and heads over the Internet to the publisher and eventually to you.

As always, to Janice, who has put up with me for more than 30 years and still laughs at most of my jokes, and to my children William and Tessa, who have progressed from our laptops to careers and lives of their own. I am proud to be husband, father, and personal computer and electronic device consultant to the clan.

Author's Acknowledgments

This book bears just one name on the cover, but that's only part of the story.

Thanks to the smart and capable crew at Wiley, including Katie Mohr and the rest of the editorial and production staff who turned the taps of my keyboard into the book you hold in the electronic device in the palm of your hand.

Also, my appreciation to long-time publishing collaborator Tonya Maddox Cupp who, once again, managed the process (and me) with grace and humor.

And as always, thanks to you for buying this book. I hope you enjoy your NOOK Color or NOOK Simple Touch eReader and proceed to support your favorite authors and publishers by filling them up with many, many books.

Publisher's Acknowledgments

We're proud of this book; please send us your comments at http://dummies.custhelp.com. For other comments, please contact our Customer Care Department within the U.S. at 877-762-2974, outside the U.S. at 317-572-3993, or fax 317-572-4002.

Some of the people who helped bring this book to market include the following:

Acquisitions, Editorial, and Vertical Websites

Project Editor: Tonya Maddox Cupp

Senior Acquisitions Editor: Katie Mohr

Editorial Manager: Jodi Jensen

Vertical Websites: Rich Graves

Editorial Assistant: Leslie Saxman

Sr. Editorial Assistant: Cherie Case

Cover Photo: © 45RPM/iStockphoto.com

Composition Services

Project Coordinator: Sheree Montgomery

Layout and Graphics: Jennifer Creasey, Christin Swinford

Proofreaders: Lauren Mandelbaum, Wordsmith Editorial

Indexer: Potomac Indexing, LLC

Publishing and Editorial for Technology Dummies

 Richard Swadley, Vice President and Executive Group Publisher

 Andy Cummings, Vice President and Publisher

 Mary Bednarek, Executive Acquisitions Director

 Mary C. Corder, Editorial Director

Publishing for Consumer Dummies

 Kathleen Nebenhaus, Vice President and Executive Publisher

Composition Services

 Debbie Stailey, Director of Composition Services

Contents at a Glance

Table of Contents

Chapter 4: Building and Managing Your Library 97

Chapter 5: Doing Tougher Stuff: Wireless, Side-Loading, Adding, Updating 129

Chapter 6: Going Online, Grabbing Mail, and Getting 'Appy with NOOK Color 143

Introduction

***I**t may seem a bit odd to some that a book needs a set of instructions, but you're no dummy: You want to get the very most out of a new technology. This book covers more than one eReader. In the early chapters of this book I explain the difference between the NOOK Color and the NOOK Simple Touch.

 This book describes two similar lines of products in the NOOK family. When I refer to *the NOOK* or a *NOOK eReader*, I'm discussing things in common to both products. When I need to distinguish between devices, I refer to the *NOOK Color* or the *NOOK Simple Touch*. And in just a few places, I mention the *NOOK Simple Touch with GlowLight.*

Foolish Assumptions

I've assumed some things about you. Nothing bad, of course:

- ✓ You have a NOOK Simple Touch or NOOK Color eReader (or are about to buy one).
- ✓ You know what an eReader is.
- ✓ You've set up and registered.
- ✓ You have access to a personal computer (and that can access to the Internet), and that you have at least a basic understanding of how to get about on the Internet.
- ✓ You have a basic understanding of how a wireless communication link is established.

Icons Used in This Book

NOOK eReaders For Dummies, Portable Edition uses a handful of special graphic elements called *icons* to get your attention. Here they are:

Here be dragons. Watch out. Be careful. Don't go there.

Here's a reminder of important stuff.

Let me tell you something you might not realize about how to use your NOOK eReader.

Ask me how to get to the post office, and I'll tell you how an internal combustion engine works.

NOOK eReader Features

Among the things both the NOOK Color and NOOK Simple Touch can do:

- ✔ Connect wirelessly to the Internet when it's near a Wi-Fi router.
- ✔ Facilitate the purchase of eBooks, magazines, and newspapers from the NOOK store.
- ✔ Link up by cable to a desktop or personal computer to allow you to side-load other reading material.
- ✔ Expand the storage space. That's a feature that isn't on many other eReaders.
- ✔ Engage in social networking, including exchanging (if you want) running commentary about the books you're reading.
- ✔ Lend some of your books to friends who have a Barnes & Noble account, or borrow reading material from them.

Here's what you *don't* get from a NOOK Simple Touch or NOOK Color:

- ✔ A built-in digital still or video camera.
- ✔ A GPS.
- ✔ A microphone.
- ✔ Projecting ability (to put an image on the NOOK screen to another device, like a television).

Where to Go from Here

You go reading, of course. And you go out of the house and take your eBook collection and your web browser and your e-mail manager with you. You go on planes, trains, and automobiles (as long as you're not the pilot, engineer, or driver). And you enjoy this newest version of a way to present one of humankind's greatest inventions: the written word.

NOOK eReaders For Dummies, Portable Edition follows the same proven formula of the other *For Dummies* books. It's for people who are smart enough to know they could use a bit of extra explanation, tips, and hints to get the most out of their new device.

Chapter 1

Getting to Know Your NOOK Color

*T*he NOOK Color can download and store thousands of full-length books, magazines, newspapers, and other publications. This very same NOOK Color can then display the material a page at a time, on a sharp screen roughly the size of a paperback book, using a very bright and colorful LCD touchscreen. In this chapter you shall explore the faces of the NOOK Color plus see a description of some of its hidden innards. Not to worry: Neither screwdriver nor hammer are required.

This first chapter introduces you to the NOOK Color, the basic LCD screen eReader model; in the second chapter you meet the NOOK Simple Touch, an E Ink reading device. Although the two electronic readers are cousins, they aren't identical in appearance, the way they work, and how you — the reader — interact with them. Later in the book I get back to their common features: storage of books and other reading material, connection to the Internet, and other features.

Getting Your Hands on the NOOK Color

In addition to your NOOK Color (see Figure 1-1), you'll see two things in the lower part of the box. See this chapter's section called "Charging up for Reading" (and Chapter 5) for the hows and whys to using these accessories:

- ✔ An AC adapter
- ✔ A specially designed USB cable

You may want to hold on to the box in case you ever decide to re-gift sell your NOOK Color. Plus, you can pack the eReader nicely if you have to send it in for repair.

All of the following descriptions are based on looking at the NOOK Color lying on its back with its top facing away from you and the bottom closest to you: very much how you look at a page from a book.

- ✔ I will call the side that has the screen the **front.** Here, of course, is the reason we are gathered together for this special occasion. See Figure 1-2. You can see on the front a button marked with the curvilinear NOOK symbol: ∩. If your NOOK Color is *sleeping* — its screen is off — the screen is also *locked* so that accidental touches don't perform actions. Press the green circle and drag it to the right to return to the last screen you were viewing.

Touch the ∩ button to wake up the device and turn on the screen. If the screen is already showing, touching the ∩ button will take you to the home screen.

Courtesy of Barnes & Noble

Figure 1-1: The handsome NOOK Color, with its open hook at bottom left and the ∩ button just below the screen.

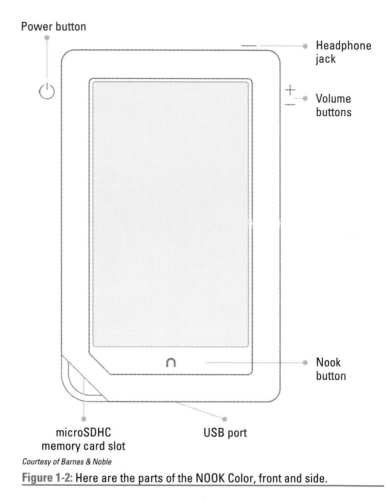

Power button

Headphone jack

Volume buttons

Nook button

microSDHC memory card slot

USB port

Courtesy of Barnes & Noble

Figure 1-2: Here are the parts of the NOOK Color, front and side.

- ✔ The side that is opposite the screen is the **back.** The NOOK Color's soft-touch back makes it easier to hold and provides a bit of a non-slip surface. See Figure 1-3. The speaker and microSD memory card slot are back here, too. Chapter 5 explains more about the memory card and its slot.

- ✔ The narrow thin side at the top I will call the **top end.** All by its lonesome, here is a headphone jack that can deliver stereo sound to a earphones or other audio devices. It is a 3.5mm jack, a standard size for modern miniature headphones or earbuds.

Back

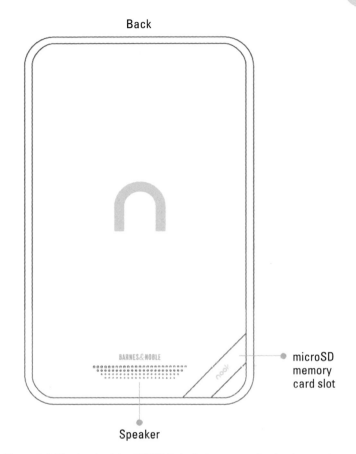

microSD
memory
card slot

Speaker

Figure 1-3: The back of the NOOK Color is home to a tiny but better-than-tinny speaker, plus a flap over the slot for a microSDHC memory card.

> ✔ The narrow thin side at the bottom, below and around the corner from the Home Button shall be dubbed the **bottom end.** Here you will find a *USB port* (a computer term for a connection point). Later in this chapter, "Charging Up for Reading" explains one way to use the port. Chapters 3 and 5 explain other ways to use it.

> ✔ The longer thin side at the left side of the front is hereby called the **left side.** The power button is here.

>> • To **turn it off,** press and hold the little rectangular button for about three seconds. Then tap the Power Off button. Why would you completely turn off

the NOOK Color? Some places demand it: airplanes during takeoff and landing and hospitals, for example.

- To **turn it on,** press and hold the silver button for three seconds (one Mississippi. . .) and release it. If you set it up to require a passcode, you'll have to type that.

- To **go into sleep mode,** press the power button and immediately release it. The eReader will stop using power, and it jumps right back to where you were the last time you were there.

✔ You will have guessed that the longer thin side at the right side of the front shall be referred to here, and just once more, as the **right side.** Here's where you find the + and – volume buttons.

Buy a small carrying case or sleeve for your tablet. It helps prevent scratches and provides some level of protection against spills or rain or falls.

Most books you buy and some you get for free come with an image of the cover along with all of the text. But some older books are just text.

Charging Up to Read

Unlike a printed book, an eReader needs batteries. The good news: The NOOK Color battery is rechargeable. The slightly less-than-good news: It doesn't have much charge when you first get it.

After you take your NOOK Color out of its box, plug your into the AC adapter and the adapter into the wall. Put some juice in the battery. See Figure 1-4.

Although you *can* connect your eReader to a USB port on a desktop or laptop computer, that may not fully charge the NOOK Color and is definitely very slow.

You want whimsy?

The design of the NOOK Color includes a cute little open notch in the lower left corner. It looks for all the world like a place to hang a hook — perhaps a mountaineer's carabiner. But please don't. The designers who worked with Barnes & Noble wanted to make their reader immediately recognizable from across the room and this was the artistic element they came up with. However, it is not intended to be used to hook the NOOK to your belt buckle or to do anything else. Although I'm sure some users will think it cute to attach some little charms or perhaps a rabbit's foot to the notch, I'd join with B&N in recommending against it: you just might end up damaging the screen.

To charge your NOOK Color, you're supposed to only use the AC adapter provided by Barnes & Noble in the package. To get the most life out of the battery, don't let it run all the way down to zero power.

You can see how much power you have by looking at the status bar at the bottom of the screen. The battery icon is fully white it's fully charged. See Figure 1-5.

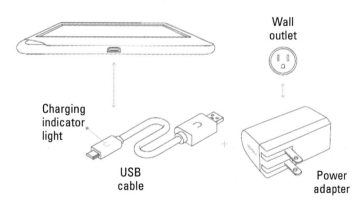

Courtesy of Barnes & Noble

Figure 1-4: The NOOK Color battery requires an AC adapter and the supplied USB cable.

Follow these steps to charge your battery:

1. **Insert the large end of the USB cable into the power adapter.**

2. **Plug the small end of the USB cable into your NOOK Color.**

3. **Plug the power adapter into a compatible electrical outlet.**

   The charging light on the USB cable shows an orange ⋂ symbol where it connects to the eReader. When it's charged, the ⋂ symbol on the cable turns green. It can take up to four hours to charge.

   Don't turn the NOOK Color off while it's charging.

4. **Unplug the power adapter from the electrical outlet.**

5. **Unplug the USB cable from your NOOK Color.**

Wi-Fi signal strength

Battery indicator

Figure 1-5: The status bar at the bottom of the screen shows the remaining charge in the battery.

At www.BN.com you can buy an adapter that lets you charge your NOOK Color from your car. Here is also where you can buy replacement or additional AC chargers and USB cables.

Registering Your NOOK Color or NOOK Simple Touch

The first time you turn on your NOOK Color or NOOK Simple Touch, devote all of ten minutes to registering it with Barnes and Noble. As you might have guessed, the process is nearly identical on the two types of NOOK devices, except that the NOOK Color does its thing in color and with video, while the NOOK Simple Touch simply uses text and icons.

If you don't, you can't use access its store (for both paid and free reading material), lend or borrow books, or get updates for your device.

 Fully charge your NOOK Color or NOOK Simple Touch before using it for the first time. Resist the urge to turn on your new eReader until you've charged it for three or four hours.

You need a working Wi-Fi system connected to the Internet to register your NOOK eReader. One quick and easy solution is to register your eReader at a Barnes & Noble store, where Wi-Fi is always available to customers who have a NOOK.

Here are the basics of getting started and registered with a NOOK Color or a NOOK Simple Touch:

1. **Turn on your fully charged NOOK.**

   On the NOOK Color only, watch a video that introduces features. The video is a good way to test the screen, processor, and audio system.

2. **Read and accept the terms of service.**

3. **Set the time zone for the current location of your eReader.**

4. **Follow the onscreen instructions to connect your NOOK to a Wi-Fi network.**

   If you have to enter a username or password, get the information from the store owner or person behind the counter.

5. **Register your NOOK to an existing Barnes & Noble account or create a Barnes & Noble account.**

Creating an account using a personal computer

You may find it easier to set up the account using a personal computer. Here's how:

1. **Open a web browser on a computer.**

2. **Go to one of these addresses:**

   * www.nook.com/setup

- www.nookcolor.com/setup

- www.barnesandnoble.com

3. **Click the Setup Account button or click Account Settings and choose a similar option.**

4. **Type the following:**

   - An e-mail address

   - A credit card number and valid expiration date

   - A billing address in the U.S., U.K., or another country in which the NOOK is marketed

The only way to connect to the Barnes & Noble website or elsewhere on the Internet from your NOOK Color or NOOK Simple Touch is through a Wi-Fi network.

These eReaders don't offer 3G or other forms of cellular connection. And the USB cable only transfers files; you can't connect through that computer to the Internet.

Using an existing Barnes & Noble account

If you already have a Barnes & Noble account, it makes great sense to use that on your new NOOK. Doing so lets you get to eBooks and periodicals already in your account and it lets you shop for new ones.

If you have an account, do this:

1. **Tap the Sign In button.**

2. **Enter the e-mail address and password for your account.**

3. **Tap Submit.**

Setting Up Your NOOK Color

You have a wide range of control over how your NOOK Color looks, feels, and acts. The Settings tool lets you customize the wireless, screen, sounds, security, keyboard, and other features.

Do this to show the Settings menu:

1. Tap the ∩ button on the lower frame of the front.

The quick nav(igation) bar opens, as shown in Figure 1-6.

2. In the quick nav bar, tap the Settings icon.

Figure 1-6: The quick nav bar on the NOOK Color is usually the fastest way to most functions.

From any customization section, you can return to the main settings screen by tapping the back arrow at the upper right of a page.

The main Settings page is divided into two parts: Device Settings and App Settings. Table 1-1 lists what you'll find in each.

Table 1-1	**Settings Page Sections**
Device Settings	*App Settings*
Device Info	Home
Wireless	Shop
Screen	Social
Sounds	Reader
Time	Search
Security	
Keyboard	

Device settings

This group of settings help you decide the personality of the hardware of your NOOK Color. See Figure 1-7. The following sections explain the Device Settings area.

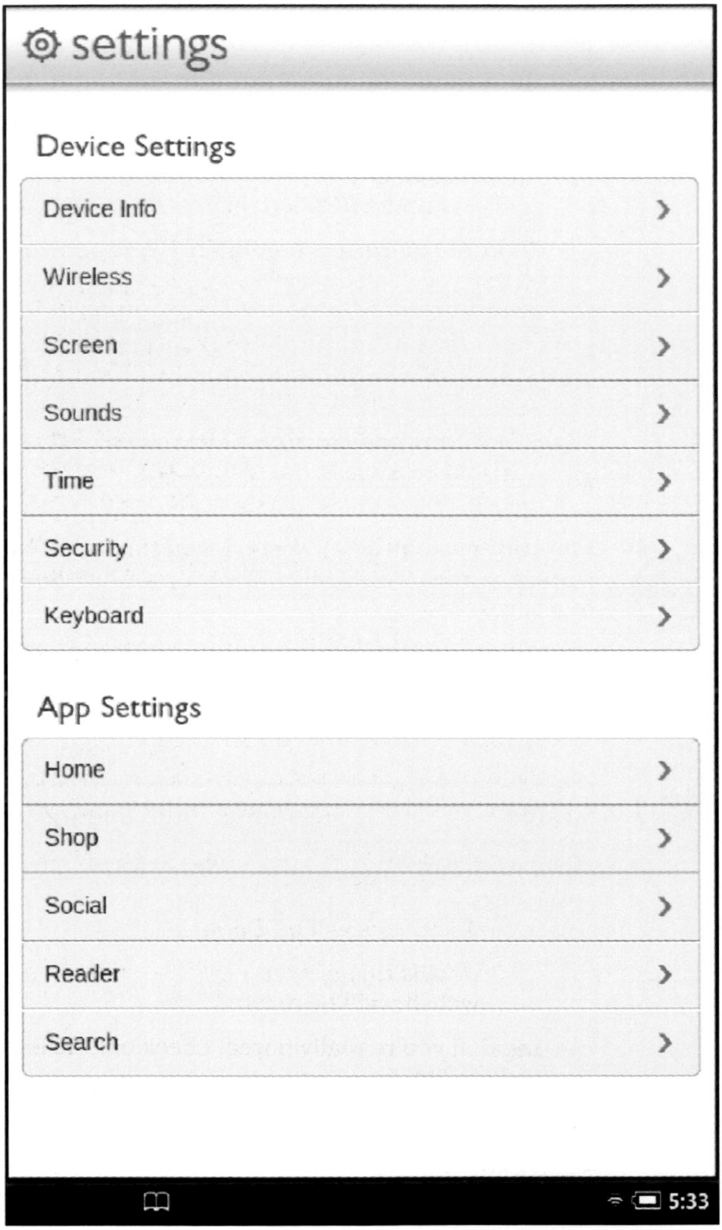

⚙ settings

Device Settings

Device Info	›
Wireless	›
Screen	›
Sounds	›
Time	›
Security	›
Keyboard	›

App Settings

Home	›
Shop	›
Social	›
Reader	›
Search	›

📖   🔋 5:33

Figure 1-7: The main settings include device and app controls.

Device Info

If you tap Device Info, you'll see these options:

- **Battery.** You can see the percentage of charge in the battery. If you're charging it up, you'll see that (along with a bright orange ∩ on the USB cable near where it connects to the NOOK Color).

- **BN Content Storage Available.** Here you will see the amount of available flash memory for books, magazines, newspapers, and apps purchased through the NOOK Store. For business reasons, Barnes & Noble has chosen to allot a bit more space in internal memory for items bought through its store.

- **Other Storage Available.** The amount of storage for items that you got from other sources (mainly files side-loaded from a desktop or personal computer).

- **SD Card.** If you've put a microSD or microSDHC card in the slot, its capacity and available storage space are listed here.

- **About Your NOOK.** Tap the arrow to see the owner and the Barnes & Noble account title, along with model number, serial number, Wi-Fi MAC address, and the operating system software version number.

- **Erase & Register Device.** Stop. Wait. *Don't tap* the big button here unless you have a real good reason to do so.

  - Personal files that you've moved to the NOOK Color will be deleted.

  - All eBooks will be deleted.

  - Details that ID your device to the Barnes & Noble website will be deleted.

- **Legal.** If you're really bored, check out the legal notices and credits.

Wireless

Tap the Wireless option to it turn, tap again to turn it off. When the Wi-Fi switch is on, you can see these things;

- All the wireless networks the NOOK Color can find in its neighborhood.

✔ Strength of the signal (a stack of curved lines). You can see what it looks like back in Figure 1-5. The more dark lines, the stronger the signal, and the faster the potential communication rate.

✔ Potentially, a lock symbol beside a network. You have to know the password to use that system. A coffee shop, fast food restaurant, or bar may give the password to customers.

I discuss wireless communication in detail in Chapter 4.

To connect to a Wi-Fi network, do this:

1. **Tap the network's name.**

2. **Tap Connect. That may be all you need to do.**

   If the network is secured, a dialog box asks for a password.

3. **Tap in the password box.**

4. **Type the password.**

5. **Tap Connect.**

Screen

Three important touchscreen controls live here. See Figure 1-8.

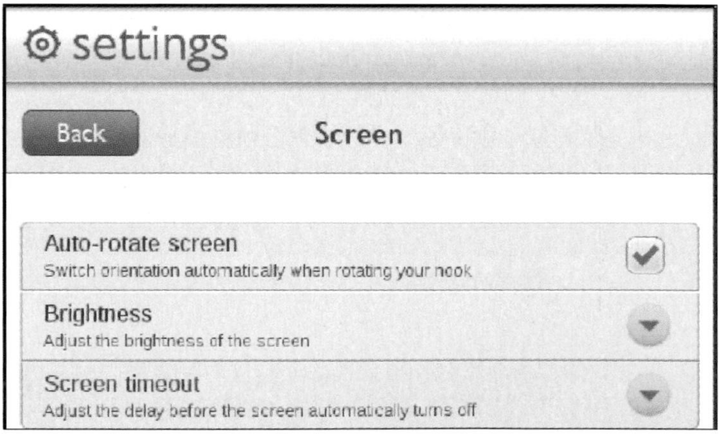

⚙ settings

Back	Screen

Auto-rotate screen
Switch orientation automatically when rotating your nook   ✔

Brightness
Adjust the brightness of the screen   ▾

Screen timeout
Adjust the delay before the screen automatically turns off   ▾

Figure 1-8: Some users don't want the NOOK Color screen to rotate.

✔ **Auto-Rotate Screen.** Sometimes pages are easier to see if you turn the eReader horizontal. You can look at your NOOK Color sideways if you tap a check mark for this option. It generally works only in the web browser, magazines, and the photo gallery. If you don't check the Auto-Rotate Screen option, the screen stays in portrait mode at all times.

✔ **Brightness.** This, of course, has nothing to do with the IQ of your NOOK Color, but rather with the intensity of its backlighting. Drag your finger to move a slider bar from dim to bright. Lower brightness levels use less battery.

A bright screen light might help in a dark room, but it might strain your eyes; a dimmer backlight may help outdoors.

✔ **Screen Timeout.** The NOOK Color turns off its screen if it doesn't get any input (taps or drags, for example). The standard setting is 2 minutes. Set the amount of time the NOOK Color should wait before turning off its screen.

The screen gets slightly dim a few seconds before it goes to sleep. When the screen shuts off, turn it back on again by pressing the ∩ button and swiping the bar from left to right.

Sounds

If only I could have installed this control on my children as they grew up; it would have added years to my life. Under Sounds, you can mute or unmute the system notification beeps and squawks made by the NOOK Color. See Figure 1-9.

⚙ settings

| Back | Sounds |

Mute
Mute sounds (except for media)

Media
Set volume for music and videos

Notification
Set volume for notifications

Figure 1-9: The Sounds setting panel lets you mute certain sounds and set the volume.

Earbud headphones help improve the sound if you're listening to music, books on tape, or videos. You can also connect your NOOK Color to an amplifier and a separate set of speakers or to external speakers with a built-in amplifier.

The various controls offered on the Sounds settings page follow:

- ✔ **Mute.** Turn on or off system notification sounds and keyboard clicks. When the check box is checked, these sounds are off; when the box is empty they'll play.

- ✔ **Media.** Press the slider bar to control the volume for music and videos. Tap OK to finalize the setting.

- ✔ **Notification volume.** Press the slider bar to control how loud system notifications (such as low battery) are. You'll hear a sample sound to indicate the loudness you've chosen. Tap OK to make the setting.

Time

Your NOOK Color's time is part of the process when you get new reading material from Barnes & Noble; some libraries that lend eBooks also use it.

You can set the clock format and time zone. Here are the options:

- ✔ **Use 24-Hour Format.** Tap in the box to turn on a 24-hour clock. I'll see you at 1730 for cocktails in the office lounge.

- ✔ **Select Time Zone.** To see all time zones around the world, tap the check box for Show All World Time Zones.

Security

Here you can apply an electronic lock to the NOOK Color itself, or to settings you make for the web browser and certain social features.

If you set it up so your NOOK Color requires a passcode, make sure it's a combination you will remember, but not one as obvious as the last four digits of your phone number or social security number. Instead, how about the last (or first) four digits of a phone number of a friend or a business not directly associated with you?

Available options follow:

- ✓ **Device Lock Passcode.** If you tap a check mark next to Require Passcode, you're asked to enter four numbers. In the future you'll have to enter that same code to turn on the NOOK Color or wake it from sleep. Use the passcode if you worry that someone might try to use your eReader: strangers or your children, for example. See Figure 1-10. To remove the passcode, tap in the box to remove check and enter the code.

  Using a passcode *doesn't* protect what's on your microSD or microSDHC memory card in the device's slot.

- ✓ **Restrictions.** You can disable your NOOK Color's social networking features, including the NOOK Friends app, connections to Facebook and Twitter, and the ability to share recommendations and quotes from an eBook. You can completely restrict web browser access, and there are separate controls for browser security elements, which I explore in Chapter 6. See Figure 1-11.

Here's how to restrict access to the social features or the web browser:

1. **On the Security settings screen, tap Restrictions.**

   A numerical keypad comes up.

2. **Tap a four-digit number.**

3. **Optional: Tap the Social check box.**

4. **Optional: Tap the Browser check box to disable the web browser.**

To change the setting, enter the passcode and tap to remove the check mark.

Figure 1-10: The code you enter is required any time you turn the NOOK Color on or wake it from sleep.

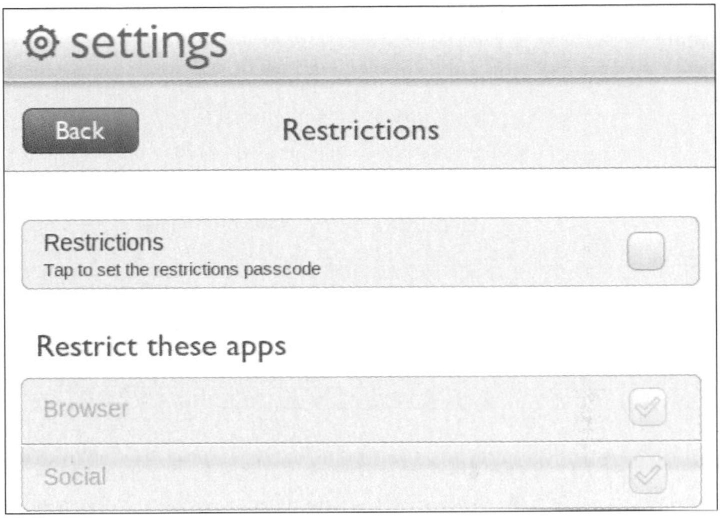

Figure 1-11: To disable the social networking features or the browser, add a restriction here.

Keyboard

The Keyboard settings page lets you customize the virtual onscreen keyboard. Tap the check box alongside any option you want to change. A check mark means that option is on; the absence of a check mark shows that the option is off.

- ✔ **Keyboard Sounds.** You can decide if you want to hear a clicking sound when you tap a key. The click is pretty quiet and confirms that you actually tapped the screen.

- ✔ **Auto-Capitalization.** You can capitalize names and initial words in recommendations and reviews.

- ✔ **Quick Fixes.** You can get help correcting some typing errors.

App settings

The app settings help you bring personality to (or take personality from) you're the NOOK Color. Get here by opening the Settings panel and tapping Home within the App Settings group. You can customize the following areas:

Home

There's no place like it.

- ✓ **Set Wallpaper.** *Wallpaper* is the background for your home screen. Your options follow:

  - **Wallpapers.** A preinstalled collection of backgrounds that come with your NOOK.

  - **Photo Gallery.** Pictures you have placed in the storage of your NOOK, including photos or drawings you have sideloaded from a desktop or laptop computer.

  - **Live Wallpapers.** Animated backgrounds you have purchased or obtained and installed in the storage of your NOOK.

- ✓ **Clear Keep Reading List.** You're asked to confirm your decision. The Keep Reading list is like the stack of books you've started reading but haven't finished; some readers flit around from title to title.

- ✓ **Clear the Daily Shelf.** The Daily Shelf is a gathering place for much of the reading material on your NOOK.

- ✓ **Configure the Contents of the Daily Shelf.** Customize the components as follows:

  - **Recommendations from Friends.** If there's no check mark here, your NOOK Color won't display suggestions from your friends on the Daily Shelf.

  - **LendMe Offers from Friends.** If there's no check mark here, lending offers won't appear in the Daily Shelf. Chapter 4 talks about lending and borrowing books.

  - **Recently Opened Library Items.** Decide whether you can see tiny covers for eBooks you've been reading lately.

  - **Recent Issues of Each Newspaper.** The standard setting shows one recent issue of each newspaper to which you subscribe; to change that, tap None, 1, 2, 3, or All.

Shop

For some, a store is home away from home. You know who you are.

✔ **Require Password for Purchases.** If you turn on this option and enter the code, you have to enter your Barnes & Noble password before buying anything from the B&N store. To get rid of the password requirement, follow these steps:

  1. **Tap to remove the check mark.**

  2. **Type your password.**

  3. **Tap OK.**

If you don't turn on Require Password for Purchases, anyone who goes to the NOOK store with your NOOK Color can buy something without knowing your shopping password.

✔ **Manage Gift Cards.** Maybe you've been with the lucky recipient of a Barnes & Noble gift card (or eGift card). See Figure 1-12. You can associate as many as three gift or eGift cards with your B&N account. Whenever you buy something from the B&N store, the balance is drawn from those cards before charging your credit or debit card.

To check the total balance of the cards associated with your B&N account, tap the Gift Cards button. To add credit to your account, do this:

  1. **On the Shop settings screen, tap Gift Cards.** A menu opens.

  2. **Tap the Add Gift Card button.** A dialog box opens.

  3. **In the fields, type the gift card information.**

  4. **If required, type your four-digit PIN.** The PIN is on the back of your card or in the e-mail that came with an eGift card.

✔ **Clear Shop Recent Searches.** This awkwardly named control will erase the list (aka *history*) of all searches you have conducted on the B&N website.

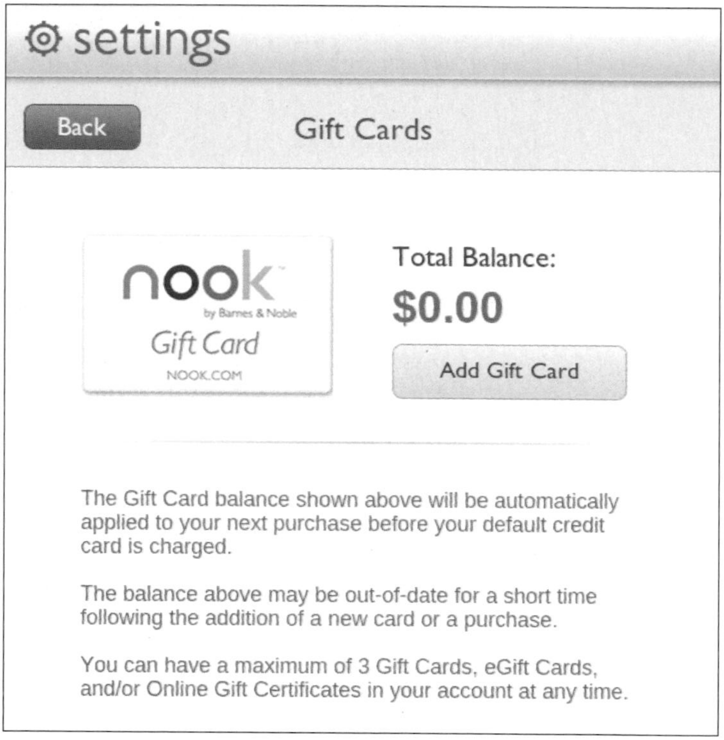

⚙ settings

Back   Gift Cards

nook
by Barnes & Noble
Gift Card
NOOK.COM

Total Balance:

$0.00

Add Gift Card

The Gift Card balance shown above will be automatically applied to your next purchase before your default credit card is charged.

The balance above may be out-of-date for a short time following the addition of a new card or a purchase.

You can have a maximum of 3 Gift Cards, eGift Cards, and/or Online Gift Certificates in your account at any time.

Figure 1-12: You can link B&N gift cards to your account as preparation for shopping at the B&N store.

Social

The Social setting is your portal to linking your Facebook, Twitter, or Google Mail accounts for easy message exchange (as well as making or accepting LendMe offers). I discuss LendMe in more detail in Chapter 4. See Figure 1-13.

These options are here:

✔ **Manage Your Accounts.** Tap the arrow to show the menu. From there you can add usernames, passwords, and some other options. Each of the services has its own button. You can allow sharing with Facebook or Twitter, and bring in contacts from Google when you link your NOOK account.

✔ **Add Facebook Friends as NOOK Friends.** If a check mark is in this box, your NOOK will automatically make NOOK friends out of your Facebook friends who have a current B&N account. You can lend or borrow books from NOOK friends. You can read more about friends in Chapter 4.

Reader

In this section you can see two options:

✔ **Animating eBook Page Turns.** If you tap a check mark for this option, pages will slide across the screen as you "turn" them, a reminder of how it used to be with books printed on sheets of paper. If they aren't sliding, pages jump from one to the next.

✔ **Enabling 2-Page Display Mode for PDFs.** If you tap a check mark for this option, you see two pages at a time of documents and books that are stored in PDF format. (I explain more about PDF files in Chapter 5.) To see two pages at a time, turn the NOOK sideways (horizontal).

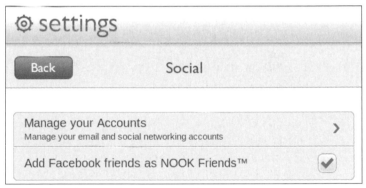

Courtesy of Barnes & Noble

Figure 1-13: The means to manage your e-mail and social networking accounts is under the Social listing of settings.

If the image won't flip when you turn your NOOK sideways, tap the ∩ button on the lower front of the NOOK frame, tap Settings in the quick nav bar, go to the Screen settings area, and turn on Auto-Rotate Screen. Some pages stay in a certain mode regardless of settings or the orientation.

Search

When you search for a file, your NOOK will always check the Library and the Shop. In the Settings panel, you can include three other locations and file types. And for the sake of privacy or excessive orderliness, you can also clear the recent history of searches. See Figure 1-14.

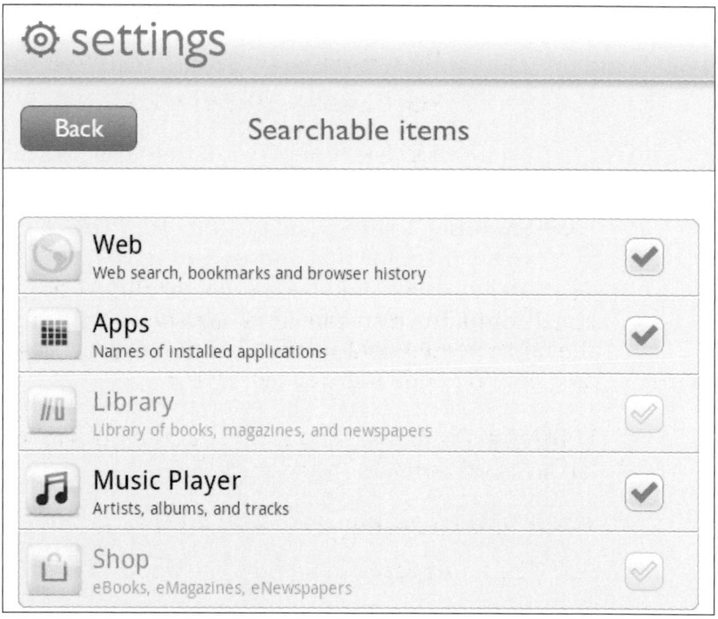

⚙ settings

| Back | Searchable items |

🌐 **Web**
Web search, bookmarks and browser history ✔

▦ **Apps**
Names of installed applications ✔

📚 **Library**
Library of books, magazines, and newspapers ✔

🎵 **Music Player**
Artists, albums, and tracks ✔

🔒 **Shop**
eBooks, eMagazines, eNewspapers ✔

Figure 1-14: You can expand or limit the areas where searches are conducted within your NOOK Color.

Here are the places where searches are conducted:

⮕ **Library.** Your collection of books, magazines, and newspapers. (Always searched.)

⮕ **Shop.** Books, magazines, newspapers, and applications available from the NOOK store. (Always searched when Wi-Fi is turned on and connected to the Internet.)

⮕ **Apps.** Applications, known as *apps,* are small programs (including games and weather checkers and note-takers). You can get them from various sources and put them on your NOOK Color.

✓ **Music.** Songs or other audio. The Search function will only find files stored in MP3 or AAC format. It finds names and titles if the file offers them.

✓ **Web.** You control bookmarks, browser history, and web searches here. Tap in the box beside Apps, Music, and Web to place or remove a check mark; only those places with a check mark will be searched.

To delete your search history, do this:

1. On the Settings screen, tap Search.

2. Tap Clear Search Shortcuts.

3. Tap OK to confirm.

Home screen

The NOOK Color's home screen is like the desktop on a personal computer. You can get to anywhere on your NOOK from the home screen, and you can put shortcuts and a personalized background on it. See Figure 1-15.

Looking at the home screen in portrait mode (taller than wide), here's what you'll find:

✓ The Keep Reading bar (across the top)

✓ The home screen panels

✓ The Daily Shelf (across the bottom)

The home screen and the Daily Shelf scroll independently of each other. You can see the Keep Reading pull-down menu on any of the three panels of the home screen. To open a book, magazine, or newspaper from the home screen or Daily Shelf, tap an item's cover. Or you can press and hold on the cover of an item to display a pop-up menu, and tap Read.

Panel indicator

Keep Reading bar

Home
screen
panels

Daily Shelf

Figure 1-15: You can change the home screen to include a personal wallpaper.

Home screen panels

The home screen has three panels that can hold shortcuts and icons for books and other reading material as well as apps. You can see only one panel at a time. In the indicator near the top of the screen, the white dot shows which of the three you're currently seeing.

- ✔ To move from one panel to another, swipe left or right across the screen.
- ✔ To make a *shortcut,* drag a book, magazine, newspaper, or document to any one of the panels. Just tap the shortcut when you want to go directly to it.

You have to turn on shortcuts. Here's how:

1. **Press the ⌒ button.**
2. **Tap Settings.**
3. **Tap Home Settings.**
4. **On the Home settings page, tap next to Show Media Shortcuts. To change your mind, tap in the box to remove the check mark.**

Get back to the home screen from anywhere by pressing the ⌒ button on the front of the device. You have to press it twice to get home if you're doing something that fills the entire screen (like playing a game or reading a kids' picture book).

The Keep Reading menu and more

The bar at the top of the home page is labeled Keep Reading. Beside the label is the name of what you were most recently reading. (It will declare None when you first start using the NOOK Color, and it may be blank if you were last viewing certain types of personal files.)

Tap any title in Keep Reading or the More menu to open the eBook.

And then there's More. Tap the More pull-down menu to see an abundance of recent reading material. To close the More menu without making a selection, tap the up arrow at the bottom of the list.

If you've read one recently, the list tells you this:

- ✔ **Books.** Titles and authors of the book most recently opened on the NOOK Color.

✔ **Periodicals.** Titles and publication dates of the most recent periodicals opened.

✔ **Files.** Titles and file types of the most recent files opened in the My Files folder.

Wallpaper

The home screen's background shows an image; borrowing from the world of computers (and old-school home decoration) this is called *wallpaper*. The NOOK Color comes with several patterns; you can also upload your own drawings or photos. The same image appears on all three of the home screen panels. I discuss how to change the wallpaper in Chapter 7.

Organizing the Daily Shelf

Give us this day our Daily Shelf, a row of books, magazines, newspapers, and apps that runs along the bottom of the home screen; items that you've recently opened, purchased, downloaded, borrowed, or otherwise received; recommendations sent by friends.

The Daily Shelf holds only one issue of a subscribed magazine or newspaper; click *The New York Times* or *Sweet Potato Monthly* to open the most recent issue.

You can move things around on the Daily Shelf:

✔ Rearrange covers if you want. Place your finger on a cover and drag it up about an inch; then drag it to a new position.

✔ Move an item from your Library to the Daily Shelf. Press and hold on an item, then drag it to the Library.

✔ Remove an item from the Daily Shelf. The item stays in your Library. Press and hold on the item. Tap Remove from Home.

✔ Move an item from the Daily Shelf to the home screen. Press and hold an item and drag it to the home screen. Or, press and hold an item on the home screen and drag it to the Daily Shelf.

Organizing the home screen

I don't let many people see the physical desktop in my office. It's a pretty scary place, with piles and piles of paper — and somewhere down there is half of a roast beef sandwich on sourdough bread with horseradish and cocktail sauce. Don't let this happen to your home screen.

You can arrange books, magazines, and newspapers dragged from the Daily Shelf to the home screen:

- **Stacking.** You can make a pile of books up to a point: You can't completely obscure any of the covers.

- **Gridding.** If you want NOOK Color to automatically arrange all the covers in a neat grid, double-tap any open area of the home screen.

You can also clean up an individual panel of the home screen. Do this:

1. **Press and hold a part of the wallpaper in the panel that you want to clean up.**

   A pop-up menu appears.

2. **Tap Clean Up This Panel.**

Frequenting Bars

Belly up to one of the bars on your NOOK Color. The special-purpose bars appear on the touchscreen as needed. The two most important bars follow:

- **Status bar.** It appears across the bottom of the screen and offers various bits of information.

- **Quick nav bar.** This bar of icons lets you quickly go to various functions of the NOOK Color.

Swipe from right to left across the status bar to return to the feature or function you were most recently using.

Status bar

The status bar's purpose is to tell you, well, the status of your NOOK Color device. The bar sits at the very bottom of the screen (just above the ∩ button). See Figure 1-16.

⊙	📖		📶 🔋 11:52

Figure 1-16: This status bar shows, from left to right, a small icon of a camera (because I captured a screen). There's an open book to allow quick access to a recent read. Icons on the far right show the Wi-Fi connection, battery life, and current time.

You may see some of the icons shown in Table 1-2.

Table 1-2   Status Bar Icons

Icon	What It Means
 ∩	New software updates have been installed.
 👥	The NOOK Friends app has new information: new contacts, new reading status, new invitations, and the like.
 📖	Tap the icon to go to the book you were most recently reading.
 P	You're listening to Pandora. (Of course, unless the volume's turned off, you already know that.) Chapter 6 explains Pandora.
 🎵	Tap to open the music player, which I explain in Chapter 6.
 ✉@	You have new e-mail.
 ⇊	Your NOOK Color is downloading books, periodicals, or apps.
 2	You have this many unexamined notifications; they could be LendMe offers or requests, recommendations from by NOOK Friends, or available updates.
 ↺	Tap to go back to a previous activity.
 📶	The more curves you see, the stronger the Wi-Fi signal. No curves? No connection.

Icon	What It Means
	A full battery means you have lots of power left. If it is half-full, that's half as good. If the battery icon is nearly empty, plug into an outlet and attach the charger. A bolt of electricity means it's charging.
	The GlowLight is on.
	You've muted the sound on your NOOK Color.

If you tap the right corner of the bar near the battery status indicator, the Quick Settings dialog box lets you change settings even more quickly. (To close the dialog box, tap anywhere outside of it.) See Figure 1-17.

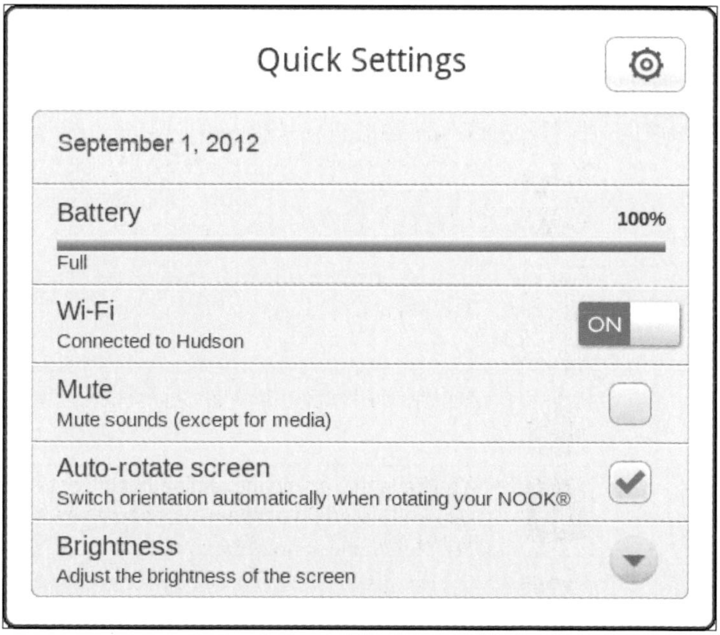

Quick Settings

September 1, 2012

Battery   100%
Full

Wi-Fi   ON
Connected to Hudson

Mute
Mute sounds (except for media)

Auto-rotate screen
Switch orientation automatically when rotating your NOOK®

Brightness
Adjust the brightness of the screen

Figure 1-17: The Quick Settings dialog box offers five of the most common adjustments.

These parts of the Quick Settings dialog box are the ones you're likely to use:

- ✔ **Battery.** See how much battery you have left.

- ✔ **Wi-Fi Toggle Switch.** Swipe or Scroll on the Wi-Fi toggle to turn the Wi-Fi system on or off. When the NOOK Color is connected to a network, you will see here the name of the network in use.

  Turn off the Wi-Fi when you don't need to use it. You'll save battery power that way.

- ✔ **Mute.** Tap the check box to mute or unmute all the sounds that notify you of something (when you tap a key, for example). Music, videos, and games aren't affected by this setting.

- ✔ **Orientation.** The screen will rotate if you turn it vertical or horizontal. Tap it to turn the auto-rotation feature on or off.

- ✔ **Brightness.** Tap to open a dialog box. Drag a slider to make the screen brighter or dimmer. A dimmer screen may be easier on your eyes and saves a bit of battery power, allowing you to read longer between recharges.

Quick nav bar

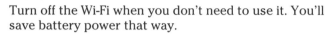

Tap the ⋂ button on the lower frame of the front to bring up the quick nav bar.

As you can see in Figure 1-18, the bar gives you quick access to seven essential components of the NOOK Color.

Figure 1-18: You can display the quick nav bar and tap one of its buttons to zoom to an important place on the eReader.

✔ **Home.** The Daily Shelf and any shortcuts you put are here.

✔ **Library.** All your reading materials are here.

- **Books.**

- **Magazines.**

- **Newspapers.**

- **My Shelves.** You can create shelves to help you organize your library. On my NOOK Color I have a Faves shelf and another that holds Lecture notes for presentations I carry on the device.

- **My Files.** Anything you have side-loaded onto your NOOK Color from a laptop or personal computer. Chapter 5 explains how to side-load.

- **LendMe.** The books that you can loan, books you've borrowed, and offers to lend or borrow. See Chapter 3 for more about LendMe.

✔ **Shop.** Takes you to the Barnes & Noble Store. I discuss the shopping experience in Chapter 3.

✔ **Search.** Takes you to the search screen so you can hunt for any file or app on your device.

✔ **Apps.** Here are pre-loaded games, multimedia utilities, e-mail, contacts programs, and apps you get from the NOOK Store.

On the original NOOK Color this option is called Extras instead of Apps.

✔ **Web.** Tapping this takes you to the Internet. If the Web button shown is pale gray *(grayed out)* and says Disabled, I expect you can guess its status. I discuss disabling the browser earlier in this chapter in the section under Security settings. You can read more in Chapter 4.

✔ **Settings.** Go to the Device and App Settings panels, described earlier in this chapter.

Chapter 2

Handling the NOOK Simple Touch

*T*he NOOK Simple Touch is the flagship model of E Ink eReaders from Barnes & Noble. It is smaller than most printed books, and simple to use, but it has serious special features. Its GlowLight adds its own built-in side lights, but it can't show videos (or most web pages).

Did I mention that it's small, lightweight, and simple to use? The NOOK Simple Touch with GlowLight was the first eReader with a built-in light for its E Ink screen; in late 2012, Amazon introduced a slightly different technology that accomplishes the same thing: Amazon Kindle Paperwhite.

The NOOK Simple touch comes in two models:

- ✔ **NOOK Simple Touch.** A 6-inch E Ink touchscreen, with built-in WiFi plus side-loading ability (which you can read about in Chapter 5). Use the USB cable that comes with the Simple Touch to recharge the battery after attaching the eReader to a powered-on desktop or laptop computer.

- ✔ **NOOK Simple Touch with GlowLight.** All of the above, plus a nifty set of tiny LED lights that you can turn on when you want to read in a dark place. The Simple Touch with GlowLight comes with an AC adapter.

Throughout this book, when I refer to the NOOK Simple Touch, the screens and actions refer to both models. In the section about the built-in lighting, I will make it clear that feature is available only on the NOOK Simple Touch with GlowLight.

Cracking Open the Box

With your NOOK Simple Touch, you get a USB cable and a booklet. See Figure 2-1. You can see a USB cable in Chapter 1.

Before you jump in, fully charge your NOOK before using it. It typically takes about three hours to fully recharge a battery. "Taking Charge" in this chapter tells you how.

Hold on to the box that your NOOK Simple Touch comes in. If (heaven forbid) you should have to send in the device for warranty service, this is premade packaging for the purpose. And it's perfect for regifting or reselling.

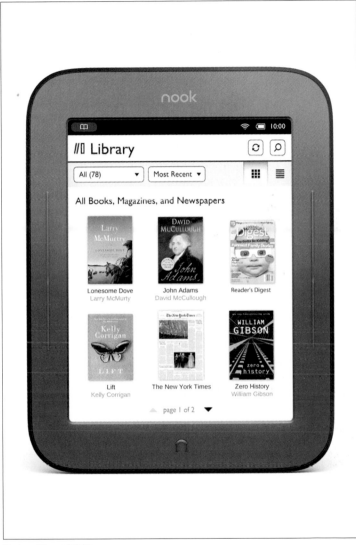

Courtesy of Barnes & Noble

Figure 2-1: The elegantly simple NOOK Simple Touch displays its library of books.

The descriptions are based on my assumption that you're looking at the NOOK as it's lying on its back with its top facing away from you and the bottom closest to you:

✔ **The top.** I wear a hat on my top end; the NOOK Simple Touch goes completely bare; there is nothing up here but a plastic shell with two dimples. The dimples are connecting points that can be used for a protective case or holder for your NOOK.

✔ **The front.** Here's home to three important items, all shown in Figure 2-2:

  • **The reading screen.** Here you can see the text of books, magazines, newspapers, and other documents in black plus 15 shades of gray.

  • **Four page-turn buttons.** The buttons are on the frame. Press < to turn back one page; press > to go forward a page. And NOOK shows righties no favoritism: Page-turn buttons are on both the left and ride side of the display screen.

  • **The ∩ button.** Also called the quick nav button. Depending on what you and your NOOK are doing, the button opens the quick nav menu, wakes it from sleep, or turns on or off the GlowLight.

✔ **The bottom.** The USB port is here. Read "Taking Charge" in this chapter for details about how to use the cable and port. Also, a pair of dimples are here; they're for a protective case or holder for your NOOK.

✔ **The back.** Here are the power button and the microSD memory card slot. See Figure 2-3.

  • **To turn it on:** Press and hold the silver button for two seconds and then release.

  • **To turn it off:** Press and hold the button for about five seconds. Tap the Power Off button on the screen to confirm.

  • **To wake it from sleep:** Briefly press the power button and release it. If you see a screensaver, your NOOK is in sleep mode.

TECHNICAL STUFF

Beam me up

Although it is referred to as a *touch-screen*, the NOOK Simple Touch actually uses an infrared sensor to detect commands you make with your fingers. Beams of *infra-red* — outside the range of human eyesight — cross the screen until they are interrupted by your finger. This is a good thing. Other designs for touchscreens place an extra layer of screen between your eyes and the text, and that doesn't always produce the best quality image with an E Ink screen.

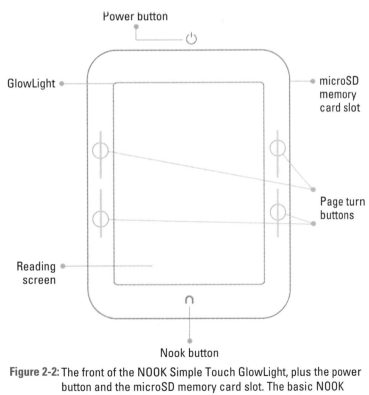

Power button

GlowLight

microSD memory card slot

Page turn buttons

Reading screen

Nook button

Figure 2-2: The front of the NOOK Simple Touch GlowLight, plus the power button and the microSD memory card slot. The basic NOOK Simple Touch is the same, without the GlowLight feature.

Power button

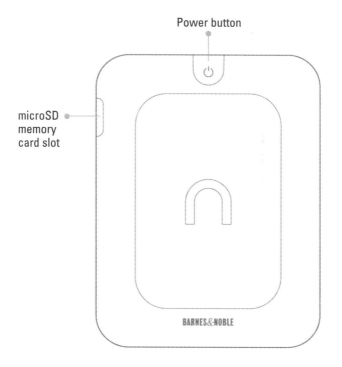

microSD
memory
card slot

BARNES&NOBLE

Figure 2-3: The back of the NOOK Simple Touch GlowLight boasts the power button, the microSD memory card slot, and a super-sized ∩ symbol.

Playing MicroSD Cards

Your NOOK Simple Touch has plenty of room for books and other reading material — but heavy users will eventually want a microSD or microSDHC memory card. The cards add a whole bunch more storage space.

Sometimes microSD memory cards are just referred to as *SD cards*. Micro relates to their size.

If you properly install a formatted memory card in your NOOK Simple Touch, you'll see two choices when you visit the device's Library:

- ✔ **My NOOK.** This is what's in the eReader's built-in memory.
- ✔ **Memory Card.** This is what's on the card in the slot.

Installing a MicroSD card

To put a memory card in a NOOK Simple Touch, do this:

1. **Make sure your hands are clean and dry.**
2. **Turn off the device.**
3. **Spread a towel or a clean cloth on a table.**
4. **Place the NOOK face down on the towel.**
5. **Find and gently lift up the small lid on the upper left side of the back of the device.**
6. **Open the package for the memory card.**

   Don't bend the card. The easiest grip is between your thumb and forefinger, with the printed logo of the memory card facing down.

7. **Carefully slide the card into the memory slot.**

   If the card doesn't slide in easily, you're probably holding it upside down or backwards.

8. **Push the card gently until it clicks into place. See Figure 2-4.**
9. **Close the lid back over the card slot.**
10. **Turn on your NOOK.**

   To remove a memory card, simply reverse the process.

Formatting the MicroSD card

Some memory cards are pre-formatted, but some aren't. The NOOK Simple Touch should recognize a memory card that isn't formatted. When it does, it shows you a message offering to fix the situation.

Here's what you need to do to format a microSD card from that point onward:

1. **Tap the Format Now button.**

   The button will be on the screen. When you tap it, the NOOK warns you that proceeding will erase the card.

2. **If you're ready, tap the Format Now button.**

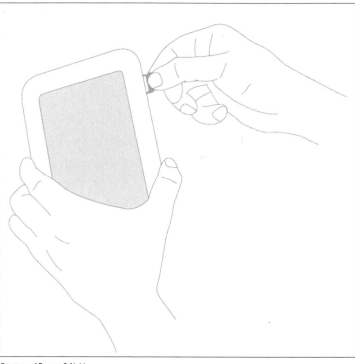

Courtesy of Barnes & Noble

Figure 2-4: An SDHC card only fits into the slot one way. Don't force it in.

Checking on storage

The Device Info screen of your NOOK Simple Touch is some-what like the instrument panel on a car: You don't often look at it, but it has a few important bits of information.

Press the ∩ button, tap Settings, and tap Device Info to see the options shown in Figure 2-5:

- **Available Storage.** Here's how much internal memory (versus *external,* or memory card) is available to hold more books.

- **SD Card.** If you've put in a microSD or microSDHC memory card, you'll see how much of its memory is available. If you haven't installed a microSD card, this section will be grayed out and a message will say that no card is inserted.

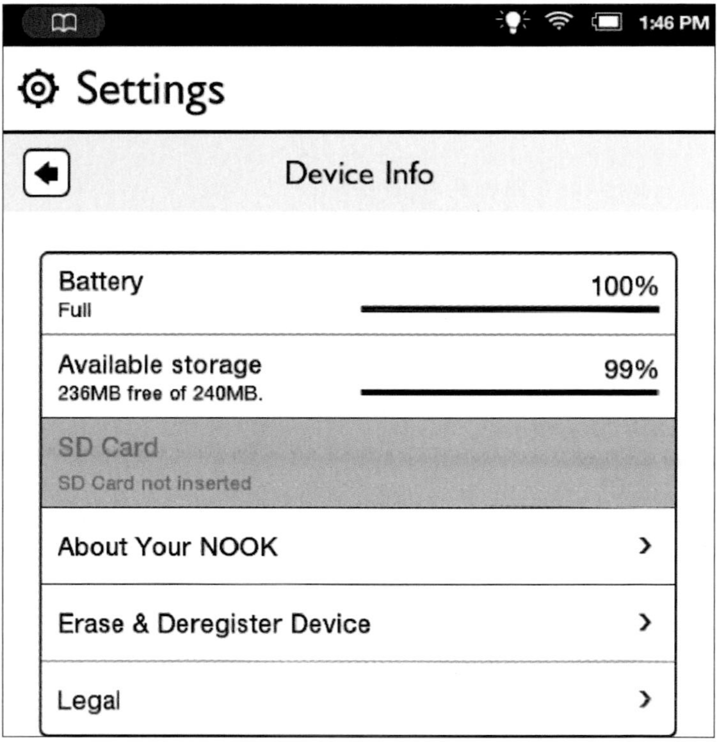

⚙ **Settings**

◀ Device Info

| Battery | 100% |
| Full | |

| Available storage | 99% |
| 236MB free of 240MB. | |

| SD Card | |
| SD Card not inserted | |

| About Your NOOK | ⟩ |

| Erase & Deregister Device | ⟩ |

| Legal | ⟩ |

Courtesy of Barnes & Noble

Figure 2-5: The Device Info screen of the Settings menu includes information about battery level, storage, and the owner of the device.

If you've put in a microSD card but it doesn't show up in this report, see if it's properly installed and has been formatted. Earlier sections in this chapter explain how to do both.

Taking Charge

Don't replace the NOOK Simple Touch battery. If the battery fails during the warranty period, you'll have to send it to a B&N repair facility; if the battery gives up once the device is out of warranty, you'll have to decide whether it makes sense to pay for a replacement. See Chapter 7 for a hint on how you may be able to extend your warranty for free.

Feeling sleepy

Consider letting your NOOK nap. Sleep mode versus turning it off has advantages. First of all, it returns to usefulness almost immediately (rather than requiring 15 seconds to start up). And second of all, if you set your NOOK to sleep and have periodicals subscriptions or preordered books, your NOOK will wake up all by itself — usually in the middle of the night — to download new content. To wake your NOOK from sleep, press the power button briefly and release it.

You can recharge your NOOK two ways. For best results, B&N recommends using an AC power adapter:

✔ Attach the supplied USB cable to your desktop or laptop computer's USB port. You can also buy any standard cable that meets the specifications: USB 2.0-compatible with a Standard A plug at one end and a Micro B at the other. The better quality cables are shielded, so look for that.

✔ Attach an AC adapter to the USB cable. The Simple Touch comes without the adapter, so you have to buy it for $10. The Simple Touch with GlowLight comes with the adapter.

Don't turn off your NOOK while it's connected to the AC adapter or to a USB power source; it won't recharge if it's turned off.

However, while a NOOK is being recharged, you can also use it to read, buy books, go to the Web, or play games. Doing so, though, will slow down the recharge process a bit since you're using some of the old electrons as new ones are poured into the battery. Okay, well, the system doesn't distinguish between old and new electrons but you get the idea.

Recharging with an AC adapter

If you have an AC adapter, follow these steps:

1. **Plug the wide end of the USB cable into the adapter.**

2. **Plug the narrow end of the USB cable into the port.**

It's the hole on the bottom edge of the NOOK.

3. **Plug the AC adapter into the wall outlet.**

A complete recharge takes about three hours. See Figure 2-6.

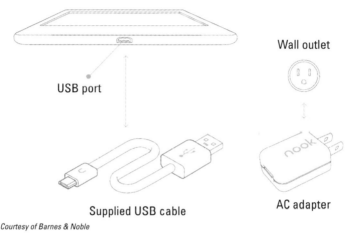

Wall outlet

USB port

Supplied USB cable

AC adapter

Courtesy of Barnes & Noble

Figure 2-6: You can recharge with an AC adapter. It comes with the NOOK Simple Touch with GlowLight. You'll have to buy one for the NOOK Simple Touch.

Recharging without an AC adapter

Your second (and slower) charging option is to use the USB cable and attach the wide end to a USB port on a laptop or personal computer. In most cases, the computer has to be running (not turned off and not sleeping) for this option to work. A full recharge from a USB source will require as much as six hours. Some newer computers have USB ports that will pass charging voltage even when they aren't turned on.

Seeing how much power is left

This isn't the most interesting reading you'll do on your NOOK, but these are important bits of information: the battery charging and the battery level indicators. When you first turn on your NOOK, or when you awaken it from a long sleep, you may see a message that the battery level reading is not available; it may take a minute or so for the system to check the tank and report a percentage.

You can look two places to see how much juice remains in the battery:

✔ **The status bar.** The bar at the bottom of the screen shows an icon that indicates power. A solid white battery is fully charged, a half-filled icon means the NOOK has used about half its power, and so on. See Figure 2-7.

Similarly, you can look at the status bar to make sure your NOOK is being recharged. In that case the battery icon will have a + sign. It can take up to 15 seconds before you can see the change onscreen.

✔ **The Settings page.** Get there this way:

1. **Tap the Settings screen.**

2. **Tap Device Info.**

3. **Tap Battery.** You can see exactly how much percentage of power is left in your battery.

Battery
indicator

Courtesy of Barnes & Noble

Figure 2-7: The NOOK Simple Touch status bar has a battery icon that shows the power level.

Here's how you can reduce the power usage: Turn off the wireless connection anytime you don't need it. Go to Settings, tap Wireless, and tap Off.

Registering Your NOOK Simple Touch

Before you can make the most out of your NOOK Simple Touch, but after you've fully charged it, register with the mothership at Barnes & Noble.

It's an easy process. Besides, otherwise you can't get any reading material from the B&N Store or use the social features. I explain the process for registering a NOOK in Chapter 1, which otherwise focused on the NOOK Color device. But just this once, can I request that you turn back the pages to Chapter 1 and follow the instructions there?

To go back to the home screen (no matter where you are), do this:

1. **Press the ∩ button.**

   The quick nav bar opens.

2. **Tap Home. See Figure 2-8.**

⌂	//▯	⌂	⌕	⌄̣Q̣̇⌄	⚙
home	library	shop	search	GlowLight™	settings

Courtesy of Barnes and Noble

Figure 2-8: This quick nav bar has the added button for the GlowLight.

Switching Up the Navigation Buttons

This section is about the physical buttons built into the frame. See Figure 2-9. The NOOK Simple Touch comes to you so the physical buttons on each side work like this: Tap either upper button to go forward a page; tap either of lower button to go back a page. But, you can change this so that tapping either of the upper buttons (left or right of the screen) go back a page, while a tap on either of the lower buttons goes forward. Why? I haven't a clue.

Here's how to perform this amazing transformation:

1. **On the Settings screen, tap Read.**

   The Reader Settings screen opens. A diagram shows you how the buttons will be reconfigured.

2. **Tap the setup that suits you best.**

   The change takes effect immediately.

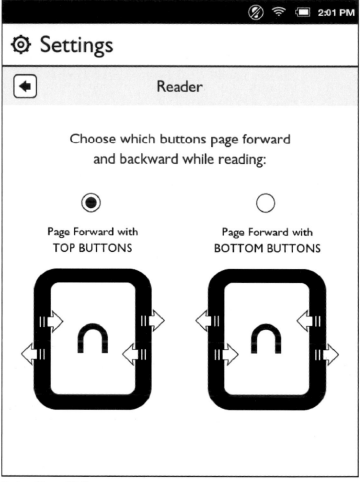

Figure 2-9: The Reader page of Settings allow you to swap the actions performed by the page buttons along the sides of the screen.

Lighting the GlowLight

The GlowLight is exactly what it sounds like: a light that glows across the screen. It lets you use the NOOK Simple Touch without the sun or a separate reading lamp. As this book goes to press, only the NOOK Simple Touch with GlowLight has, you know, the GlowLight.

You have two ways to turn the GlowLight on or off:

✓ **Press and hold the ∩ button until the light comes on.** If it's already on, press and hold the ∩ button until it turns off. The little light bulb icon in the status bar at the top of the screen will appear when the GlowLight is turned on. See Figures 2-10.

✓ Or follow these steps:

    1. **Press the ∩ button.**

    2. **Tap Settings.**

    3. **Tap GlowLight.**

    4. **To turn it on, tap the check box; to turn it off, tap the check box to remove the check mark.**

    5. **Push the black bar in the Brightness slider left or right.**

       You can adjust the brightness this way. See Figure 2-11. You can, of course, only adjust the brightness of the GlowLight if it's on.

GlowLight is on

Courtesy of Barnes & Noble

Figure 2-10: The light bulb in the status bar at the top of the screen reminds you that the GlowLight is on.

Courtesy of Barnes & Noble

Figure 2-11: The GlowLight settings panel lets you adjust the built-in lighting.

Erasing and Deregistering

Careful! Following the steps in this section leads to all kinds of information being erased from your eReader. If you really want to proceed, here's how to erase and deregister a NOOK Simple Touch or a NOOK Color:

1. **Make sure your NOOK is connected to a Wi-Fi network and linked to the Internet.**

2. **Press the ∩ button.**

   The quick nav bar opens.

3. **Tap Settings.**

4. **Tap Device Info.**

5. **Tap Erase & Deregister Device.**

   A dialog box appears. Consider again. You'll lose all your information on your eReader!

6. **Tap Reset NOOK.**

The device will reboot and look like it did the first time you turned it on.

Keep in mind the following:

- If you want to **re-register with your existing account** (and get back the content that you had already bought from Barnes & Noble), follow the onscreen instructions and enter your account name and password.

- If you want to **register with a different existing account** (and load content from that account), enter the name and password.

- If you want to **create a new account,** follow the onscreen instructions.

Screening Your Settings

The Screen settings page shows a couple options:

- **Screen timeout.** Tap the down arrow to decide how much time must pass (without you touching it, of course) before the NOOK Simple Touch into sleep mode.

- **Screensaver.** When your NOOK Simple Touch goes to sleep, it shows the screensaver.

Here's what to do if you want to use a custom image for your screensaver:

1. **Connect your NOOK Simple Touch to the computer by the USB cable.**

2. **Use Windows Explorer or Mac Finder to find the screensavers folder on your NOOK.**

3. **Create a new folder there.**

Name it something like MyScreensavers or Pictures.

4. **Drag the image from your PC to the folder you just created.**

The file must be one of these formats: GIF, JPG, or PNG.

5. **Tap to make it active.**

Here's how to choose one of the screensavers that's already on your NOOK:

1. **Press the ∩ button.**

   The quick nav bar opens.

2. **Tap Settings.**

   The Settings screen opens.

3. **Tap Screen.**

4. **Tap the Screensaver button.**

5. **Tap the option you want:**

   - **Authors**

   - **Nature**

   - **Custom folder** (if you created one) and then the image

Controlling Your Password

This section applies to both NOOK Color and NOOK Simple Touch.

If you choose, you can add one more level of protection between your NOOK and your Barnes & Noble account. You can require the Barnes & Noble store to ask for your secret password before something can be bought.

Here's how to require a password for buying:

1. **Tap the ∩ button.**

   The quick nav bar opens.

2. **Tap Settings.**

   The Settings screen opens.

3. **Tap Shop.**

4. **Tap the check box beside Require Password for Purchases.**

   A dialog box opens and asks you to enter your password to confirm that this is really what you want to do.

5. **Tap in the password field and type the password.**

6. **Tap OK.**

   The Require Password for Purchases check box isn't available if you already require a password. To remove the password requirement, follow Steps 1-3. After you type the password, you'll be able to tap the check box.

Chapter 3

Reading, Gesturing, and Socializing

*T*he NOOK Color and NOOK Simple Touch have a form of touchscreen: a system that detect touches. The NOOK Color has an LCD screen, which is like a tiny television. On the other hand, the NOOK Simple Touch uses the elegant and simple E Ink display.

How do you deal with these newfangled things called *tablet* and *touchscreen?* You tap, swipe, pinch, zoom, or press. And somehow it works. This chapter applies to both the NOOK Color and the NOOK Simple Touch devices.

The NOOK Simple Touch can't show videos and action games. The NOOK Color has a relatively full-featured Web browser while the NOOK Simple Touch doesn't.

Letting Your Fingers Do the Walking

The following sections explain the basic gestures available to you on your NOOK eReader; I point out the few cases where the NOOK Color and NOOK Simple Touch are different.

Because the devices are similar, some of the figures show the NOOK Simple Touch and others show the NOOK Color.

Using menus

Here's how to use the menus on the touchscreen:

- ✔ Tap a menu choice with a > to the right to see submenus.
- ✔ Tap the < to go back up to the previous level.
- ✔ Tap a down arrow to see the menu choices.
- ✔ Swipe up or down to see on a menu to see more choices. You'll know there are more options when you see a scroll bar running up and down the right side of the menu. (Touching the scroll bar itself doesn't move anything around.)
- ✔ If you see On or Off for menu choices, tap the option once to change the selection.

If a menu item is *grayed out* (shown in gray instead of dark black), it means you can't select it.

Tap: Simple Touch and Color

A quick strike with the tip of your finger: A tap is the most common gesture on the NOOK. When I say *tap,* I mean a gentle prod. Think of tapping on a window with a finger — which is pretty much what you're doing. See Figure 3-1.

On a NOOK Simple Touch and NOOK Color, do this:

- ✔ Tap an icon on the quick nav bar or on the home screen to open a menu or a book.
- ✔ Tap a menu option to choose it.
- ✔ Tap the right or left side of an eBook page to go forward or backward a page.

On a NOOK Color only, do this:

- ✔ Tap an app to use it.
- ✔ Tap an item on a web page to select it.

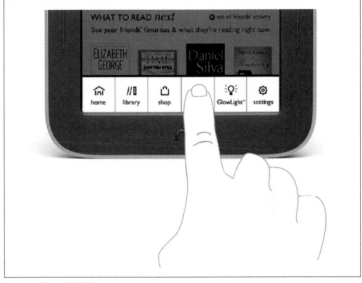

Courtesy of Barnes & Noble

Figure 3-1: A tap is like a mouse click.

Don't slam the screen. Don't use a pen, stylus, or chisel to touch your screen: Scratches and damage could result. The touchscreen is meant to be lovingly fondled by human fingers, although it would also respond to toes.

Double-tap: Simple Touch and Color

Knock, knock. Bet you figured this one out, right? Two quick strikes by the tip of your finger. The action performed by this gesture depends on the application you are using on your eReader. Here are some possibilities:

On a NOOK Simple Touch and NOOK Color, do this:

> ✔ Double-tap a book or periodical in the onscreen library to open a window with details about the item.

On a NOOK Color only, do this:

> ✔ Double-tap a picture in the Gallery to zoom in on the picture; double-tap again to return to the original view.

✔ Double-tap an empty place on the home screen to arrange book covers and other items into a neat grid. (I would pay a small fortune for a similar electronic genie to clean up my office.)

Press and hold (long press): Simple Touch and Color

This gesture is also called a *long press*. Touch a finger to the screen and hold it there for about two seconds. Eventually, you lift your finger from the screen after finishing a gesture such as dragging. I tell you this just as a precautionary measure so that you don't feel you have to walk around for the rest of the week with your finger glued to the touchscreen. See Figure 3-2.

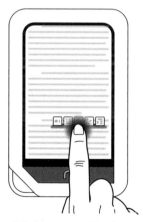

Figure 3-2: A press-and-hold gesture brings up a menu related to whatever you're identifying with your finger; shown here is the step to display the Reading Tools on the NOOK Color.

On a NOOK Simple Touch and NOOK Color, do this:

✔ Press and hold to open a pop-up menu (also known as a *context-sensitive menu*).

✔ Press and hold on a word in an eBook to select text to copy, highlight, share, or to look up in the dictionary or (on the NOOK Color only) an Internet source.

Swipe: Simple Touch and Color

Swiping means sliding your finger across the screen as though you were cleaning the dust off your desktop. And just to mix things up, you may sometimes see the word *slide* used instead of *swipe*. See Figure 3-3.

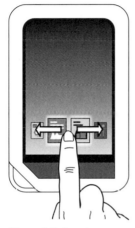

Figure 3-3: A swipe moves through a set of icons or moves an item left or right.

On a NOOK Simple Touch and NOOK Color, do this;

✓ Swipe across the row of lock icons at the bottom of the NOOK Simple Touch (across the unlock bar to unlock the NOOK Color) when you first turn it on, or anytime it's in sleep mode.

✓ Swipe left or right to turn pages in an eBook.

✓ Swipe left or right to move options on the home page.

✓ Swipe left on the status bar (the strip at the top of the screen) to go back to your previous activity.

Scroll: Simple Touch and Color

Scrolling is a form of swiping, except that you move your finger up or down on the screen to go through a list. Think of it as using the up or down arrow keys on a computer keyboard. See Figure 3-4.

Courtesy of Barnes & Noble

Figure 3-4: A scroll is like a vertical swipe, shown here on a NOOK Simple Touch.

Drag: Color

When you drag on a touchscreen, you are — in an electronically metaphoric way — touching an object and dragging it somewhere else. Touch an object and keep your finger on it as you drag it to where you want it; when your finger has arrived, lift it from the screen to leave the object in its new location.

Pinch: Color

A *pinch* requires two fingers. Lay each finger on the touchscreen and bring them toward (or away from) each other. Most people use their thumb and pointer finger, on either hand. See Figure 3-5.

- ✔ Pinch your fingers together to shrink an image — a book cover or a photo, for example.

- ✔ *Pinch out* (spread your fingers apart) to zoom or enlarge an image — to look at a map with more detail, for instance.

Figure 3-5: Pinch to zoom in or out on text or an image on the NOOK Color.

You can't always pinch something onscreen.

Playing to Type: Keyboard

What keyboard, you ask? Not to worry: When you need to fill out a form, set up a Wi-Fi connection, choose a book, or enter your credit card number, the NOOK eReaders bring forth an electronic keyboard. See Figure 3-6.

The NOOK eReaders are great for e-mail and web browsing, but write a book on your a desktop or laptop computer.

Revealing the keyboard

To bring up the keyboard, tap anywhere on a screen where you're being asked for text or numbers. For example, look for a text box on a web page. If you come to a page that requires numbers, in many cases you will see a box of numbers to tap.

When you finish typing, tap Go. Apps or websites may use different keys. For example, Go is the standard key to send your characters, but some pages substitute Search, Return, or Enter. See Figure 3-7.

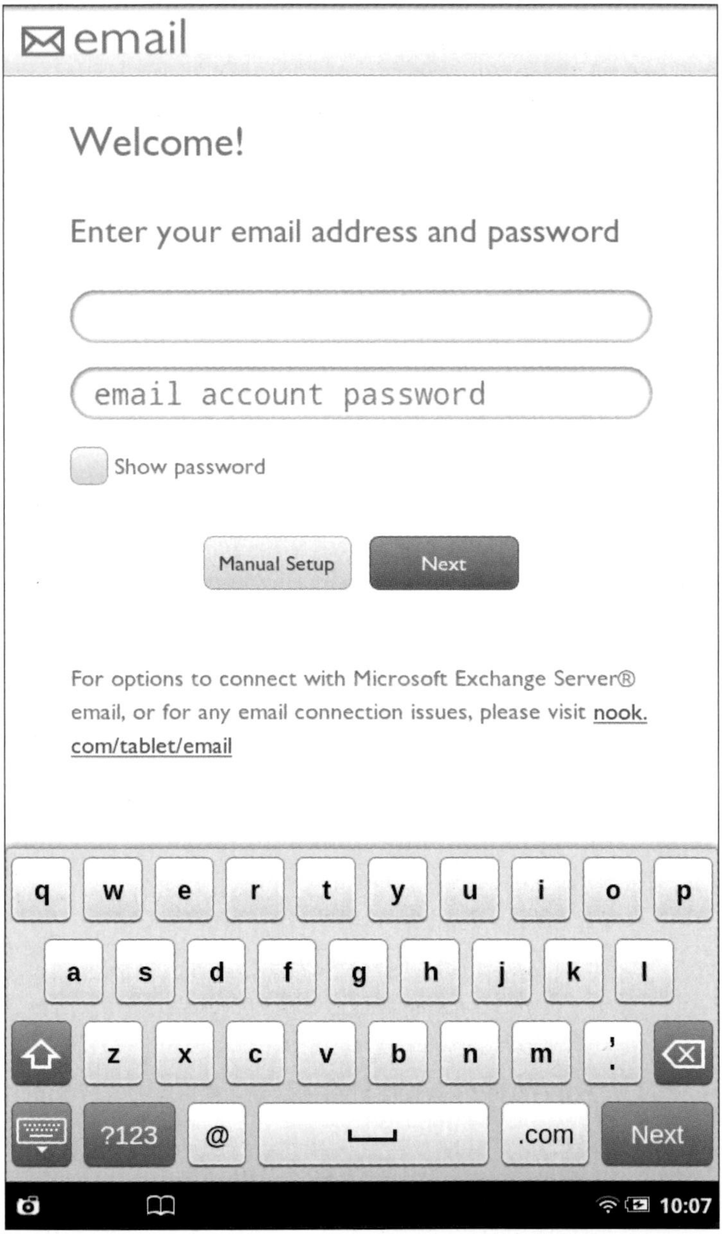

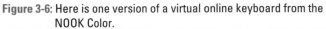

> ✉ email
>
> ## Welcome!
>
> Enter your email address and password
>
> (_____)
>
> (email account password)
>
> ☐ Show password
>
> [Manual Setup]   [**Next**]
>
> For options to connect with Microsoft Exchange Server®
> email, or for any email connection issues, please visit nook.
> com/tablet/email
>
> | q | w | e | r | t | y | u | i | o | p |
> |---|---|---|---|---|---|---|---|---|---|
> | a | s | d | f | g | h | j | k | l | |
>
> ⇧ z x c v b n m ; ⌫
>
> ⌨ ?123 @ ⎵ .com Next
>
> 📷   📖   🔋 10:07

Figure 3-6: Here is one version of a virtual online keyboard from the
NOOK Color.

Courtesy of Barnes & Noble

Figure 3-7: On this keyboard (for a search function on the NOOK Simple Touch), the action button is marked Search.

On the NOOK Color, if the text box is too small to tap or hard to read, make it bigger by pinching out on the screen. (Alas, on the NOOK Simple Touch, what you see is what you will almost always get; screens won't pinch, period.)

Typing numbers or symbols

Keep in mind these tips when you need numbers or symbols:

- ✔ To **show numbers,** tap the button marked ?123. Tap the ABC key to return to the alphabet.

- ✔ To **switch to a symbols keyboard,** tap ?123 and then tap ALT. Tap the ABC key to return to the alphabet.

- ✔ To **enter non-English characters or accent marks,** press and hold a letter on the keyboard. A pop-up window offers options. Tap the one you want.

Closing the keyboard

The keyboard will disappear after you tap Go (or Return, Enter, Search, or similar command).

You also can close the keyboard by tapping the Cancel button, to the left of the ?123 button:

✔ On the NOOK Simple Touch, it's called Cancel.

✔ On the NOOK Color, it's an icon of a keyboard with a tiny down-facing arrow.

Reading Books, Magazines, and Newspapers

I'm going way out on a limb here and guessing that you didn't buy your NOOK for use as a high-tech paperweight. You want to read books, magazines, and newspapers. Good news! That's exactly what it was designed to do.

This chapter concentrates on reading books. Your NOOK Color or NOOK Simple Touch can handle these file types (or *formats*):

✔ EPUB

✔ PDFs

 Calibre will *convert* (change) a files to EPUB format. Calibre is a free program that you put on your desktop or laptop computer. You can get it at `www.calibre-ebook.com`.

Opening a book

If this is the first time you've turned on a NOOK Color or a NOOK Simple Touch — fresh out of the box and but all nicely charged up — then you've got to stock the shelves. I show you how to do that in Chapter 3. Here, I assume that you've downloaded some books or periodicals from the B&N store or dragged some content from your laptop or personal computer.

 Naturally enough, you begin by opening a book. If the cover's on your home screen, tap it. Or press the ⋂ button to go open the quick nav bar and tap Library. Then tap the cover of the title you want to read. It's really that simple. See Figure 3-8.

On the NOOK Color, look at the Keep Reading section of the status bar. Tap the title to reopen a book or document that you've started reading.

Courtesy of Barnes & Noble

Figure 3-8: One way to open a book is to tap its cover in the Library, shown here on a NOOK Color.

You can always stop reading a book partway through and open another book (and another and another). The most recently opened books are listed in the I'm Reading section for quick access, but even if they aren't, you can return to the exact page you last read when you reopen a book.

Turning pages

Don't lick your finger and try to turn a page. Instead, try these methods:

- Tap anywhere along the right edge of the page to turn to the next page. Tap anywhere along the left edge of the page to turn back to the previous page.

- Swipe to the left to turn to the next page. To swipe left, place your finger on the right side of the page and slide it or flick it quickly to the left. Swipe to the right to go back a page.

- On the NOOK Simple Touch only, press one of the four page-turn buttons. Two are along the frame on each side of the front.

- Use one of the advanced Reading Tools. What are they? Read on.

 Most books that you buy will allow you to jump from chapter to chapter and search the text. Some publishers, though, may offer more limited features.

Designing your own pages

When you buy an actual printed book, someone else has chosen the font and size. With (most) eBooks you can decide on those elements yourself.

Adjusting text: Simple Touch and Color

Here are some of the things you can do with *most* books:

- **Typeface**. Also known as *font*. Select the design you prefer. NOOK eReaders have different styles, some of which are shown in Figure 3-9.

- **Size**. Adjust the size of the type, on a relative scale from small to very large.

  ✔ **Line spacing.** Choose the amount of space between each line of type.

  ✔ **Margin size.** Set the margins to either add space around the sides of the text or to spread text out to fill the screen.

Changing Text Theme: Color

The NOOK Color offers six themes that may be helpful in unusual lighting conditions. The choices, shown in Figure 3-10, include:

1. **Press the ∩ button.**

2. **Tap Settings.**

3. **Tap Screen or Display.**

4. **Tap a theme.**

   Night is helpful when you're trying to read at night or in dark places.

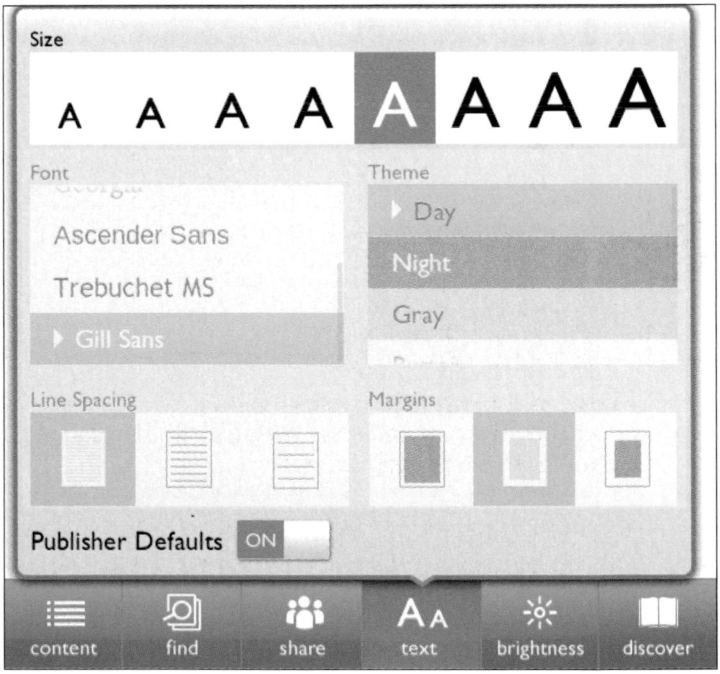

Figure 3-9: The Text menu lets you choose an eBook's typeface and text size.

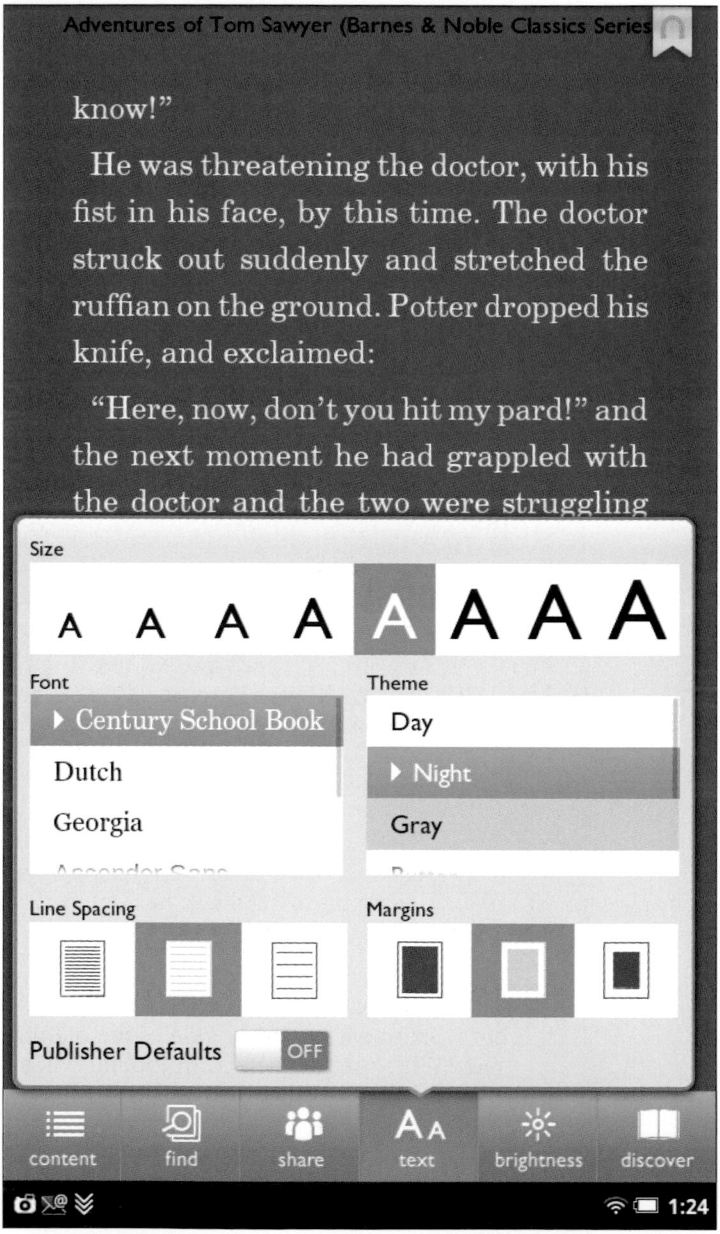

Adventures of Tom Sawyer (Barnes & Noble Classics Series)

know!"

He was threatening the doctor, with his fist in his face, by this time. The doctor struck out suddenly and stretched the ruffian on the ground. Potter dropped his knife, and exclaimed:

"Here, now, don't you hit my pard!" and the next moment he had grappled with the doctor and the two were struggling

Size

A A A A A A A A

Font

▶ Century School Book

Dutch

Georgia

Theme

Day

▶ Night

Gray

Line Spacing

Margins

Publisher Defaults OFF

| content | find | share | text | brightness | discover |

1:24

Figure 3-10: On the NOOK Color, I chose the Night theme, which puts white text against a nearly black page.

Everybody turn to page 5

A sentence that's on page 100 of a hardcover book might be on page 194 in the eBook (if you chose normal-sized Century Schoolbook) or on page 327 (if you chose Gill Sans typeface in large size with double-spacing and wide margins). A single page may spread across several screens or digital pages. You may "turn" page 47 two or three times before moving on to page 48 on the eReader.

Has someone referred to a particular passage? You can find it in the eBook. Use the search or find functions of the NOOK Color or NOOK Simple Touch.

Marking, copying, and searching text: Simple Touch and Color

You can tell the NOOK Color or the NOOK Simple Touch to select a word, sentence, or paragraph and then share those pearls of wisdom through e-mail or social networks. You can also, on either NOOK, look for a dictionary definition of a word. On the NOOK Color you can venture out on the web to do some more advanced research.

Here's how to work with text:

1. **With something to read on the screen, use your finger to press and hold on a word.**

   The word will be highlighted in color on a NOOK Color and a gray box on the NOOK Simple Touch. A vertical bar will appear on either side of the highlight. At the same time, the text selection toolbar will appear on screen. See Figure 3-11.

2. **Drag the first bar to the beginning of whatever you want to highlight. Drag the second bar to the end of the passage.**

3. **Tap the selected text.**

   The text selection toolbar opens.

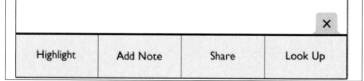

Tess of the d'Urbervilles (Barnes & Noble...

XXII

THEY CAME DOWNSTAIRS YAWNING next morning; but skimming and milking were proceeded with as usual, and they went indoors to breakfast. Dairyman Crick was discovered stamping about the house. He had received a letter, in which a customer had complained that the butter had a twang.

"And begad, so 't have!" said the dairyman, who held in his left hand a wooden slice on which a lump of butter was stuck. "Yes – taste for yourself! "

Several of them gathered round him; and Mr Clare tasted, Tess tasted, also the other indoor milkmaids, one or two of the milking-men, and last of all Mrs Crick, who came out from the waiting breakfast-table. There certainly was a twang.

The dairyman, who had thrown himself into abstraction to better realize the taste, and so divine the particular species of noxious weed to which it appertained, suddenly exclaimed –

×

| Highlight | Add Note | Share | Look Up |

Courtesy of Barnes & Noble

Figure 3-11: A section of text has been marked on this screen of the NOOK Simple Touch.

4. **Tap an option:**

  • **Highlight.**

  • **Notes.** See following for more on this option.

  • **Share.** The text can go to friends you already have an e-mail address for in Contacts. You can tap the Add Contacts button to add a person. See Figure 3-12.

- **Look Up.** Use the dictionary to search for a definition. On the NOOK Color you can tap the Google or Wikipedia icon to look online. (You must have an active Wi-Fi connection to the Internet.) See Figure 3-13.

- **Find.** On the NOOK Color, tap here to search the current book for other instances in which the selected word appears.

If you decide not to perform any of the options, just tap on the page outside of the text selection toolbar.

On the NOOK Color, you can change the highlight color. Follow Steps 1-4 and then do this:

1. **Tap the highlight after the toolbar has closed.**

2. **Tap the color you want.**

   On the NOOK Simple Touch, you have a choice of gray, gray or, if you prefer, gray.

Notes are helpful for lots of reasons. To add a note, follow Steps 1-3 (just before) and then do this:

1. **Tap Note.**

2. **Tap Add Note.**

3. **Type your note.**

4. **Tap Post Note (NOOK Color) or Done (NOOK Simple Touch).**

   An icon shows up in the page margin when you make a note. To read the note, tap the icon.

You also can edit or get rid of a note.

1. **When you're looking at a note, tap the Edit button.**

   If the note isn't already open, tap the note icon in the margin.

2. **Type the changes.**

3. **Tap Post Note (NOOK Color) or Done (NOOK Simple Touch).**

To see all the notes in an eBook, do this:

1. **Tap any page in the book.**

   The Reading Tools open.

2. **Tap the Contents icon.**

3. **Tap the Notes & Highlights tab.**

👥 Share [✕]

| Recommend | › |

| Post Reading Status | › |

| Rate and Review | › |

| Like on Facebook | › |

| LendMe® | › |

| View Friends' Activities | › |

Figure 3-12: You can share wise words by tapping the Share button on the NOOK Simple Touch screen.

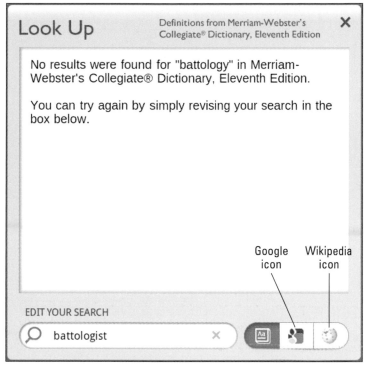

Look Up

Definitions from Merriam-Webster's Collegiate® Dictionary, Eleventh Edition ✕

No results were found for "battology" in Merriam-Webster's Collegiate® Dictionary, Eleventh Edition.

You can try again by simply revising your search in the box below.

Google icon   Wikipedia icon

EDIT YOUR SEARCH

battologist

Figure 3-13: Here the NOOK Color can't define "battology," which everyone knows refers to the unnecessary repetition of the same words or ideas. I mean, everyone knows. Everyone.

Using reading tools

Several powerful gizmos are grouped in the reading tools. The tools allow you to move quickly through a book, search for particular content, and adjust the way the pages appear.

To open the reading tools, tap near the center of the page.

NOOK Color reading tools

The NOOK Color reading tools are on a virtual shelf above any word or phrase you've highlighted. See Figure 3-14. The tools follow:

- ✔ **Content.** Open a table of contents for the book, with the current chapter highlighted. You'll also see three tabs:

  - **Contents.** Chapter titles, sometimes with subsections. In most books you can jump to a section by tapping the title or subsection name.

  - **Notes & Highlights.** A list of any passages you've highlighted or written notes about in the current book. Again, you can jump to any of them by tapping on the item.

  - **Bookmarks.** All the bookmarks you've set in the current book. Jump to any of the pages by tapping it.

- ✔ **Find.** Look for a word or phrase anywhere in the current book. Type what you're looking for, then tap Search in the lower right corner.

Before you can use e-mail or social network services, you must first link your NOOK Color or NOOK Simple Touch to your Facebook and Twitter accounts (see later in this chapter) or add some e-mail accounts to the Contacts list on the eReader.

verses of the recitation. Ten blue tickets equaled a red one, and could be exchanged for it; ten red tickets equaled a yellow one; for ten yellow tickets the superintendent gave a very plainly bound

Bib rtl ce th sy to the industry and application to memorize two thousand verses, even for a Doré Bible?[4] And yet Mary had acquired two Bibles in this way—it was

Figure 3-14: The NOOK Color reading tools lie just a tap away within a book.

✔ **Share.** Got something you'd like to tell others? A submenu offers these choices:

- **Recommend.** Praise a book or document. You choose what avenue to use.

- **Rate and Review.** Send your comments and a rating for display on www.BN.com. The rating can be posted to Facebook or Twitter.

- **Post Reading Status.** Tell others how far you've gotten in a book on Facebook or Twitter. I'm really not sure why, but someone must be interested.

- **Like This on Facebook.** Post a status declaring that you like this book.

✔ **Text.** This is the gateway to adjusting font style, size, line spacing, margins, and themes.

✔ **Brightness.** Reveal a slider that you can drag to adjust the backlight (on a NOOK Color). Tap anywhere other than the slider to close the window.

✔ **Discover.** See customized book recommendations.

On the NOOK Color, above these basic tools is a *slider;* it's a gray line with a blue dot somewhere along it. The dot shows your current place in the book. To move forward or backward quickly, drag the slider right or left. If you're reading a loaner book, you'll also see a button at the right that lets you buy your own copy.

You may also see a small blue flag all the way to the right end of the slider. Tap that flag to see recommendations for similar books or special content that comes with the electronic edition.

The NOOK Color has an archive function; it's in the Library section.

1. **Press the ∩ button.**

2. **Tap Library.**

3. **Press and hold on the cover of a book or periodical.**

   A pop-up menu opens.

4. **Tap Archive.**

   To retrieve a book, press and hold its cover and select Unarchive.

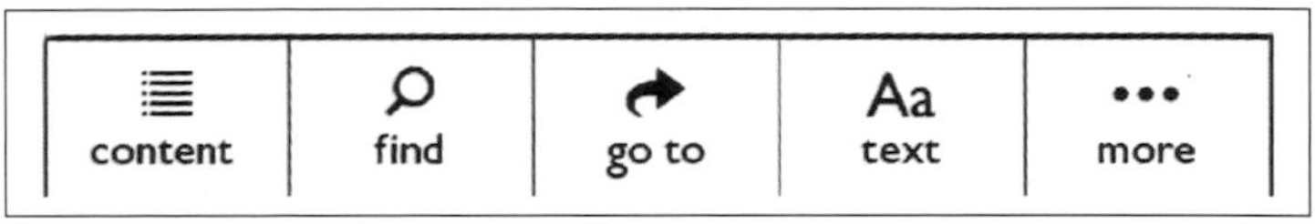

| ☰ content | 🔍 find | ↪ go to | Aa text | ••• more |

Figure 3-15: The reading tools on the NOOK Simple Touch place social media features one level beneath the More button.

NOOK Simple Touch reading tools

The NOOK Simple Touch reading tools are similar. See Figure 3-15. Content and Find are the same on the NOOK Simple Touch as they are on a NOOK Color. The rest differ:

✔ **Go To.** Skip forward or backward to a specific page in the book. Press and hold the bar that spreads from left to right. Or, tap the Go to Page button and type a page number.

✔ **Text.** Adjust font style, size, line spacing, and margins.

If you tap the More option, you can read details like ratings by B&N users, reviews, and related titles. Buttons you can press here on the NOOK Simple Touch include these:

✔ **Read.** Return to a book.

✔ **LendMe.** If the book is eligible, you can offer it by tapping here.

✔ **Share.** Accept a request to borrow the book, or share your thoughts or rating. Some of the options are the same as on the NOOK Color (Recommend, Post Reading Status, Rate and Review, and like on Facebook). Some other options appear:

 • **LendMe.** Start the LendMe program for this title.

 • **View Friends' Activities.** See recommendations, shared quotes, and the other bookish activities of your NOOK friends.

✔ **Archive.** Put the current title into deep storage and free up some space on your eReader. Get the eBook back anytime:

 1. **Connect to a Wi-Fi system.**

 2. **Tap the ⋂ button.**

 The quick nav bar opens.

3. Tap Library.

4. Tap the Archived menu.

5. Find the book you want to retrieve.

6. Tap Unarchive. It's downloaded to your Library.

Bookmarking your spot

An electronic bookmark works just like a piece of paper stuck between the pages of a paper book: It allows you to quickly open to a particular page.

To bookmark the page you're reading, tap in the upper right corner of the page. A small ribbon icon will appear in the corner of the page.

To see all the bookmarks in a book, do this:

1. Tap the center of the page to open the reading tools.

2. Tap the Contents icon.

3. Tap the Bookmarks tab.

Keep these bookmark shortcuts in mind:

✓ **Jump directly to any bookmarked passage or page:** Tap the bookmark. See Figure 3-16.

✓ **Close the bookmark list without visiting a bookmark:** Tap anywhere on the page of the book outside the list of bookmarks.

✓ **Remove a bookmark on the current page:** Tap the ribbon in the upper right corner of the page.

✓ **Clear all the bookmarks in a book:**

1. Tap the Contents icon in the reading tools.

2. Tap the Bookmarks tab.

3. Tap the Clear All button in the lower left corner of the bookmarks list.

4. Tap OK.

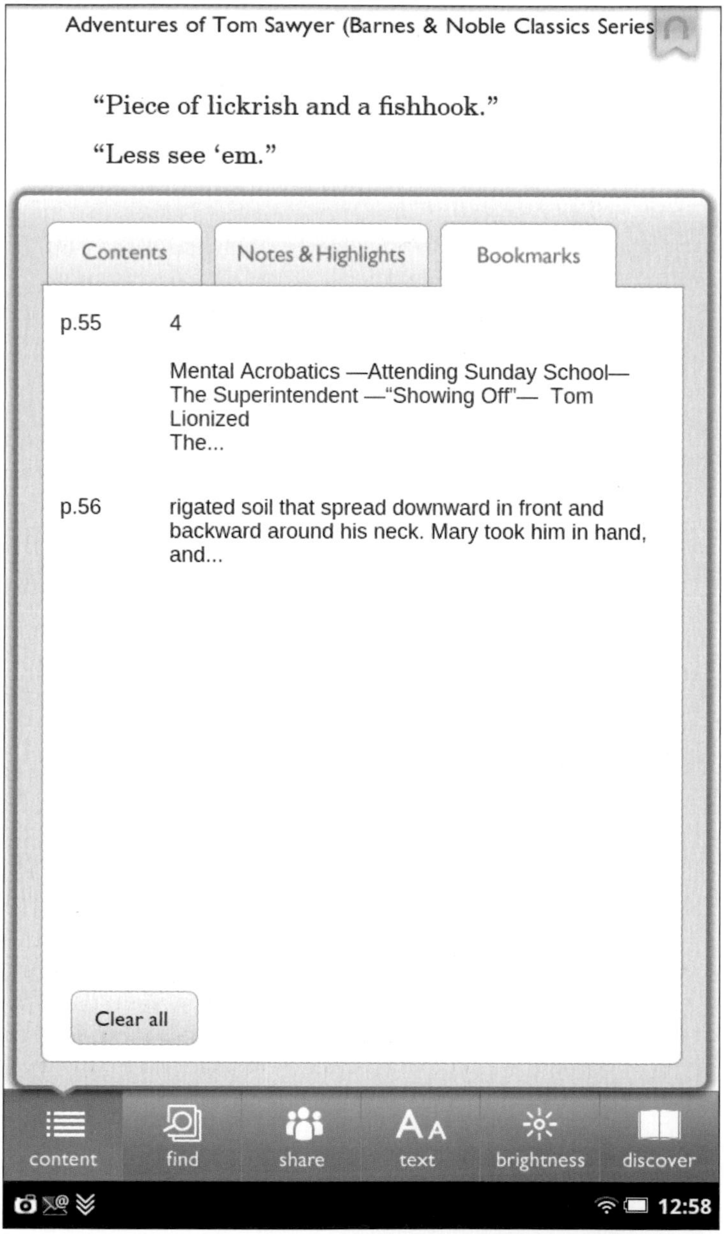

Adventures of Tom Sawyer (Barnes & Noble Classics Series

"Piece of lickrish and a fishhook."

"Less see 'em."

| Contents | Notes & Highlights | Bookmarks |

p.55   4

Mental Acrobatics —Attending Sunday School—
The Superintendent —"Showing Off"— Tom
Lionized
The...

p.56   rigated soil that spread downward in front and
backward around his neck. Mary took him in hand,
and...

Clear all

| content | find | share | text | brightness | discover |

12:58

Figure 3-16: A list of bookmarks is stored with a book on the NOOK Color.

Reading a magazine

Magazines are where the NOOK Color and NOOK Simple Touch differ. On the NOOK Color, you may be able to zoom in on photographs or illustrations, and some offer enhanced features (like interactive graphics, videos, and web links). See Figure 3-17.

Magazines on a NOOK Color

Most magazines offer a format with a choice of two views for reading:

- ✔ **Page view** looks like the printed magazine.
    - To move through the magazine: Swipe your finger along the *thumbnail* (small) pictures. Tap a picture to jump directly to it.
    - To move forward a page: Tap the right side of the screen. Tap the left side to go back a page.
    - To make the thumbnail pictures reappear: Tap in the middle of the screen.
- ✔ **Article view** shows just the articles without illustrations or photos.
    - To move forward a page: Tap the right side of the screen. Tap the left side to go back a page.
    - Tap the Contents icon: You can then see and tap the cover, the table of contents, or a specific article.

Magazines on a NOOK Simple Touch

Most magazines on the NOOK Simple Touch are similar to a book. When you're reading one, you can tap in the middle of the page to use the reading tools, including Contents and Go To. Some periodicals may offer their own table of contents with links to special features. However, all the images are in black and white.

Reading a newspaper

Newspapers around the world offer electronic versions; in most cases you can get your daily paper anywhere you can sign on to the Internet using Wi-Fi. See Figure 3-18.

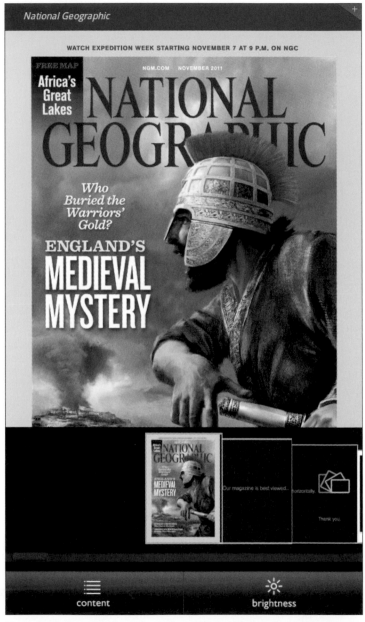

Figure 3-17: One of the best examples of fine magazine design translated to an eReader is the venerable *National Geographic,* shown here on a NOOK Color.

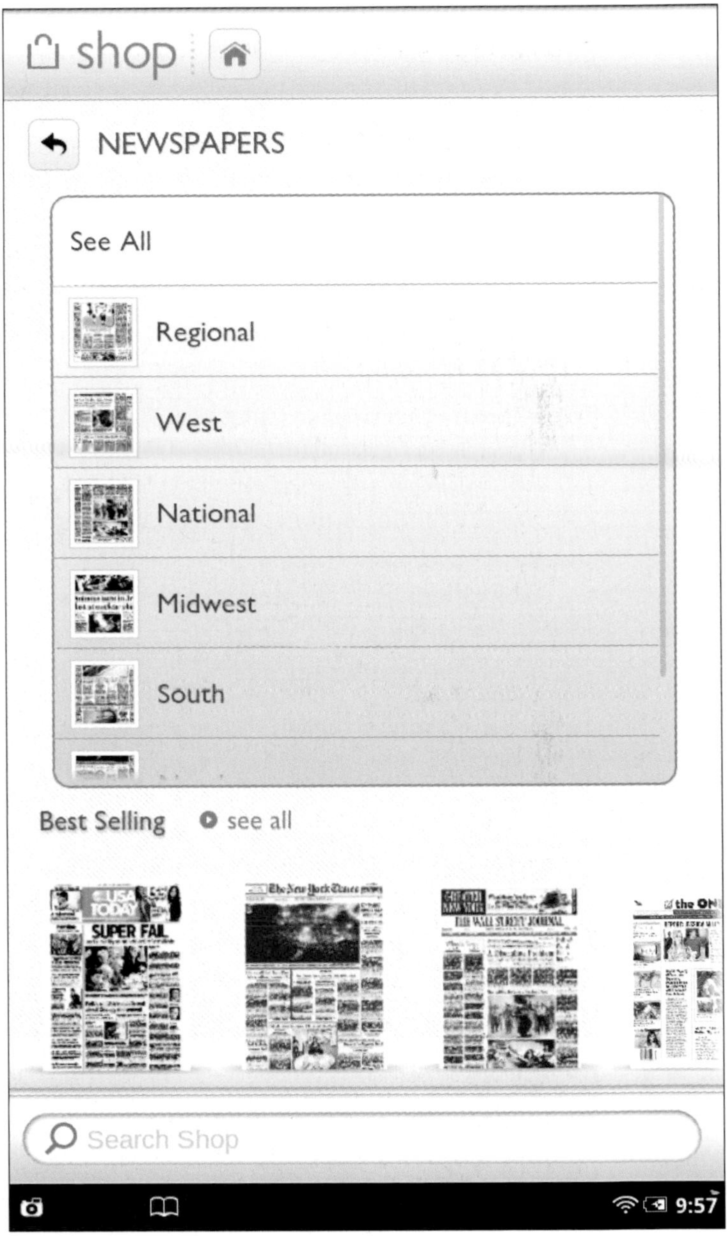

🛍 shop 🏠

🔙 NEWSPAPERS

See All

Regional

West

National

Midwest

South

Best Selling ▶ see all

🔍 Search Shop

📷 📖 📶 🔋 9:57

Figure 3-18: The NOOK store holds a collection of newspapers unmatched by any brick-and-mortar newsstand.

With either device, a newspaper is kept in the Newsstand or Magazines section of your Library. On the NOOK Color, it also appears on the Daily Shelf.

- ✔ To **open a newspaper,** tap its cover.
- ✔ To **read an article,** tap its headline or the introductory paragraphs.
- ✔ To **share an article or add notes,** tap in the middle of the page and choose the right options from the reading tools.
- ✔ To **bookmark a page,** tap in the upper right corner of the page.

To turn to the next page of a newspaper, do any of the following:

- ✔ Tap along the right edge of the screen.
- ✔ Swipe your finger from right to left across the screen.
- ✔ Swipe your finger from low to high on the screen.

To go back a page in a newspaper, do one of these actions:

- ✔ Tap along the left edge of the screen.
- ✔ Swipe your finger from left to right across the screen.
- ✔ Swipe your finger from high to low on the screen.

Reading to the kids

The NOOK Color offers NOOK Kids, children's books with special features for young readers (and those of us who sit by their side as they discover the joys of reading). Some kids' books become animated when you tap the screen. Others read aloud portions of the book. See Figure 3-19.

NOOK Kids picture books work only on the NOOK Color and NOOK Tablet. You can generally get classic children's literature (not picture books) in eBook form for all NOOK eReaders.

- ✔ Tap the Read To Me button to have the story read to you (and the nearest child) as the pages are turned. This assumes, of course, that the option is available. You may just have to read it yourself.

✔ Move forward page by swiping to the left. Go back a page by swiping to the right.

✔ To skip from one part of a kids' book to another:

1. **Tap the white arrow at the bottom of the screen. You'll see small pages** *(thumbnails)* **from the book.**

2. **Slide your finger right or left across the thumbnails to go to the page you want to read.**

3. **Tap the thumbnail of a page to jump to it.**

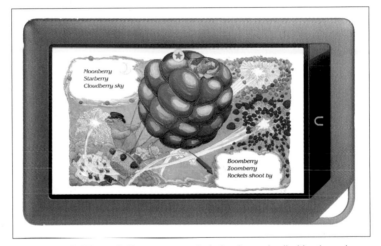

Figure 3-19: Children of all ages cannot help but be enthralled by the color — and other features — of a picture book on the NOOK Color.

Adjusting NOOK Color screen brightness

Adjusting the screen brightness can make reading more comfortable. To adjust the brightness, do this:

1. **Tap the center of the page.**

    The reading tools appear.

2. **Tap the Brightness icon at the right end of the toolbar.**

3. **Drag the slider left (dimmer) or right (brighter).**

4. When the brightness is to your liking, tap the center of the page.

Making NOOK Friends

Barnes & Noble has something called NOOK Friends that allows registered users to borrow or lend certain reading material associated with a NOOK account.

You need certain things to become a NOOK Friend:

- ✔ A Barnes & Noble account. Chapter 1 tells you how to do that if you haven't already.
- ✔ An e-mail address that's in the Contacts list on a NOOK device. (Tap Contacts, tap Add Contacts, and fill in the fields.)
- ✔ One person or the other must accept a NOOK Friends invitation sent by the other. (Sending or accepting an invitation sets up a relationship between you.)

Now, how about learning what your NOOK Friends are doing? Updates are sent when a NOOK is connected to the Internet through Wi-Fi, so you may be out of touch if a NOOK Friend is offline.

Here's how to check for any book in your Library or Barnes & Noble store:

1. Double-tap the book cover.

2. Tap the Share button.

The Share dialog box opens.

3. Tap View Friends' Activities.

See Figure 3-12 earlier in this chapter.

If you're reading the book, you can do this:

1. Tap in the center of any page of the book.

The reading tools open.

2. Tap More.

3. Tap Share.

Managing Your Social Life

The NOOK Simple Touch and the NOOK Color can link to social media including Facebook, Twitter, and Google accounts. Using these services allows you to share quotes, recommendations, and reading status with your friends.

 Your NOOK must have its Wi-Fi system turned on and you must be connected to the Internet to participate in social media or book sharing. The following steps also assume that you already have an account with Facebook, Twitter, and Google. If you don't, use your personal computer to visit their respective websites and sign up.

To manage your electronic social life on the NOOK Simple Touch, do this:

1. **Press the ∩ button.**

   The quick nav bar opens.

2. **Tap Settings.**

   The Settings page opens.

3. **Tap Social.**

   See Figure 3-20.

4. **Tap the right-facing arrow next to Link to Facebook, Twitter, and Google.**

5. **Tap in your username and password.**

Facebook and Twitter

Follow these steps for either Facebook or Twitter:

1. **Tap that the Facebook or Twitter logo.**

   Your NOOK is now linked to your Facebook or Twitter account.

2. **Type the e-mail or phone number associated with your account.**

3. **Type your Facebook or Twitter password.**

4. **Tap the Login button.**

If you're using Facebook, you're ready. If you're using Twitter, you're asked if you want to allow NOOK by Barnes & Noble to connect to your account.

5. Tap the Allow button.

If you post to Twitter from an eBook (assuming your accounts are linked), your NOOK will put a link to the referenced book in your message.

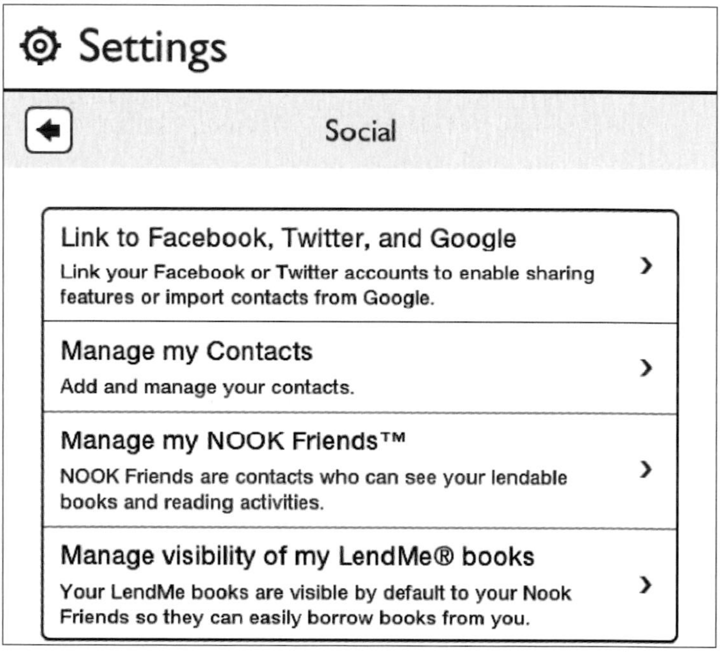

⚙ Settings

[◀]   Social

Link to Facebook, Twitter, and Google
Link your Facebook or Twitter accounts to enable sharing
features or import contacts from Google.   ❯

Manage my Contacts
Add and manage your contacts.   ❯

Manage my NOOK Friends™
NOOK Friends are contacts who can see your lendable
books and reading activities.   ❯

Manage visibility of my LendMe® books
Your LendMe books are visible by default to your Nook
Friends so they can easily borrow books from you.   ❯

Courtesy of Barnes & Noble

Figure 3-20: The Social page, shown here on the NOOK Simple Touch, is where you manage your links to social networks, contacts, and NOOK Friends.

Google

To use Google, follow these steps:

1. Tap the Google logo.

That links your NOOK to your account.

2. Type the e-mail associated with your account.

3. **Type your Facebook or Twitter password.**

4. **Optional: Tap to put a check mark in the Remember Me box.**

   If you turn on Remember Me, your e-mail and password will be filled in the next time you come to this screen.

5. **Tap Sign-in.**

   The Google account management page opens.

6. **Tap Grant Access.**

7. **Tap Manage My Contacts.**

   Tap the option to add, delete, or edit the information for any contacts you have on your reading NOOK.

If you accept a request from someone to become a NOOK Friend, that person's information is automatically sent into the contacts list.

Adding a contact

To manually add a contact, do this:

1. **On the Settings screen, tap Social.**

2. **Tap Manage My Contacts.**

   You'll see all your contacts. If you want to see only your Google contacts or your NOOK Friend, tap the pull-down menu in the upper left corner and tap that option.

3. **Tap Add Contact.**

4. **The Contact Information page opens.**

5. **Tap in the fields and type first name, last name, and e-mail.**

6. **Optional: To send an e-mail invitation to become a NOOK Friend, tap the Invite as NOOK Friend check box.**

7. **Tap Save.**

   The contact's name is added to the list titled Sent Invitations.

Deleting a contact

To remove a contact, do this:

1. **On the Settings screen, tap Social.**

2. **Tap Manage My Contacts.**

3. **Tap the person's name.**

    The Contact Information page opens.

4. **Tap Delete This Contact.**

Inviting someone to become NOOK Friends from Contacts

You've already got this person's name in Contacts. Now you want to be NOOK Friends, too. Do this:

1. **On the Settings screen, tap Social.**

2. **Tap Manage My Contacts.**

3. **Tap the person's name.**

4. **Tap in the Invite as NOOK Friend check box.**

5. **Tap Save.**

    The contact's name is added to the list of Sent Invitations. Whether your invitation is accepted or rejected, you'll see the response from your erstwhile friend in the Contacts listing.

Viewing or editing contact information

You can't change a contact that was imported from your Google account. Those, you have to change directly in the Google profiles that you can reach from your computer.

Follow these steps to update something, if need be:

1. **Press the ∩ button.**

    The quick nav bar open.

2. **Tap Settings.**

3. **Tap Social.**

4. **Tap Manage My Contacts.**

5. Tap the person's name.

6. Tap the field you want to edit.

7. Optional: To add a second address, tap the Add New button; to remove an e-mail, tap the minus symbol next to the address. You must have at least one e-mail address for each contact.

You'll find your NOOK Library stocked with books available for lending, as well as those that have been loaned out. See Figure 3-21.

Manage NOOK Friends

Handle NOOK Friends by tapping the NOOK button and then Settings; tap Social to get to the Manage My NOOK Friends page. Here you can extend (or take back) an offer of NOOK friendship as set up under a Barnes & Noble account.

You'll find three tabs:

✔ **Friends.** The contacts who have accepted your offer of friendship, or those whose invitations you accepted. Swipe your finger on the touchscreen to scroll through the list. Tap a name to learn about books (from the Barnes & Noble store) in your friend's collection.

To remove someone from the list, do this:

1. Press and hold on the name.

2. Tap Remove Friend.

✔ **Requests.** Invitations you've gotten but that you haven't confirmed. Tap Accept to add this person as a NOOK Friend, or tap Reject not to.

✔ **Sent.** Contacts to whom you've sent an invitation to become a NOOK Friend. If one of your invitees accepts the offer, their name will move to the Friends tab.

To cancel an invitation, do this:

1. Press and hold on the name.

2. Tap Cancel Invite.

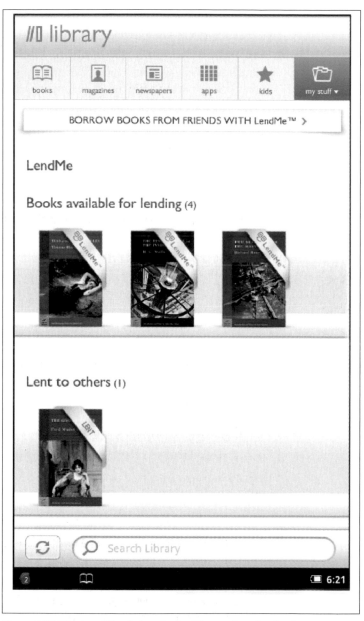

Figure 3-21: The LendMe shelves in the Library show books that you can loan or those you're borrowing.

Inviting a contact to become a NOOK Friend

To invite a contact to become a NOOK Friend, do this:

1. **Press the ∩ button.**

   The quick nav bar open.

2. **Tap Settings.**

3. **Tap Social.**

4. **Tap Manage My Contacts.**

5. **Tap the + button.**

   You'll see your existing contacts.

6. **Tap the Invite button next to the right name.**

   An invitation goes out.

 If you haven't already *imported* (copied) contacts from a Google account, you'll see a Setup Account button in the dialog box. Tap it to open the Social Settings menu to link your NOOK to your Google account.

Manage visibility of my LendMe books

Your LendMe books are visible to your NOOK Friends. If you want to change that, follow these steps:

1. **Press the ∩ button.**

   The quick nav bar open.

2. **Tap Settings.**

   The Settings screen opens.

3. **Tap Social.**

   The Social Settings screen opens.

4. **Tap Manage Visibility of My LendMe books.**

   The language here is a bit confusing.

5. **To hide your books from NOOK Friends, leave the Show All My Lendable Books to My NOOK Friends check box *without* a check mark.**

   If you *do* tap and put a check in the check box, your NOOK Friends will be able to see your books.

If you want to make individual decisions about which books will be visible to your friends, do this:

1. **Tap a check mark in the Show All My Lendable Books to My NOOK Friends check box.**

2. **Tap in the box beside each book on your list.**

3. **Tap either Show or Hide for each book.**

Chapter 4
Building and Managing Your Library

. . . .

In This Chapter

▶ Finding your way around

▶ Shopping at Barnes & Noble

▶ Lending and borrowing

▶ Mastering your digital domain

▶ Shopping at other stores

▶ Using text, spreadsheet, and other files

. . . .

*T*his chapter explores how you can stock your NOOK's shelves with bestselling books, great classics, and specialized or obscure titles of interest only to you. You can read how to do the same with magazines and newspapers. I also tell you how to find free books. And finally, I explain how to move documents from your computer to your NOOK.

Knowing What Goes Where

The NOOK Color and Simple Touch are made for and sold by Barnes & Noble, but you can get books from sources other than B&N. However, you must set up an account with Barnes & Noble, whether or not you ever plan to buy anything from the store.

Things are stored this way:

> ✓ The books and periodicals you buy from the NOOK store go into your NOOK Library.
>
> ✓ Books and documents that you've side-loaded from a laptop or personal computer go into My Documents. Get to it by tapping Library, then My Files, and then My Documents.

The list is out there on the Internet, and you can visit it any time by signing in to your B&N account. See Figure 4-1.

Shopping at B&N on Your NOOK

The NOOK Color can show some pictures or videos that you put into its memory, run a few apps, and play a few games. The NOOK Simple Touch — as impressive as it is — is an eReader only.

1. **Make sure you're connected to the Internet by a Wi-Fi connection.**

   You are if you can see the Wi-Fi signal at the top status bar. If you aren't, go to Chapter 5 for directions.

2. **Press the ∩ button.**

   The quick nav bar opens.

3. **Tap Shop.**

   Make your way past the ads.

4. **When you get to a book you want to buy, tap the button that has the price.**

5. **Tap Confirm if you're sure you want to buy it.**

   Your credit card (the one you associated with your Barnes & Noble account) is charged.

When you buy a book or publication it immediately starts coming *(downloading)* to your. It should take a minute at most. If the download is interrupted, it can restart later without your being charged again.

Courtesy of Barnes & Noble

Figure 4-1: The books, magazines, and newspapers you buy from the NOOK store are put in the Library. This collection is on a NOOK Simple Touch with GlowLight.

In some rare cases you may need to unlock a book or periodical purchased through Barnes & Noble. You'll be asked to enter your B&N password.

 ✔ Your name

 ✔ The e-mail address that you use with your B&N account

 ✔ The credit card number used to make the purchase

Using NOOK in a B&N retail store

When you turn on your NOOK in the store, the device asks if you'd like to connect to the in-store network. See Figure 4-2. Tap either Connect or Dismiss. If you tap Connect, you get special privileges:

 ✔ A free pass to read most NOOK eBooks for one hour per day.

 ✔ Content and offers available only to NOOK owners using the in-store network.

Return to the store's home page by tapping the Shop icon. It's in the upper left corner of the NOOK Color screen, and in the upper right corner of the NOOK Simple Touch.

If you have any questions about setting up an account or have trouble using your NOOK eReader, you can call Barnes & Noble customer service at 1-800-843-2665.

Browsing categories

To browse lists and categories of books and periodicals, tap the Browse button on the Shop screen.

The NOOK Color's screen is a bit livelier, but the same basic elements are there. The store's home screen shows the following categories:

 ✔ Books

 ✔ Magazines

 ✔ Newspapers

✔ Kids

✔ Apps (NOOK Color only)

✔ Music and video (NOOK Color only)

Courtesy of Barnes & Noble

Figure 4-2: When your NOOK is at an actual Barnes & Noble store, it will feel right at home.

Searching for and buying books

I recommend setting up your NOOK so that it requires your B&N account password before you can buy anything. I explain how to do this later in this chapter, in the section titled "Shopping Securely."

To look for and buy a particular book or periodical, do this:

1. **Tap the search field.**

   The field is at the bottom of the NOOK Color; it's on the upper right of the NOOK Simple Touch.

2. **Type the title, author, or subject you'd like to explore.**

3. **Tap Search.**

   If your search results don't all fit on the screen, drag your finger up or down the screen.

4. **Tap a listing to read more.**

5. **Tap the green button (NOOK Color) or a gray box (NOOK Simple Touch) with a price.**

   See Figure 4-3. Buying an app from the NOOK store is like buying an eBook. I discuss apps in more detail in Chapter 6.

Buying magazines or newspapers

You can buy individual issues of a newspaper or magazine, or you can subscribe. The best deals come with longer-term subscriptions. And it bears mentioning one more time: The NOOK Color uses 16 million colors while the NOOK Simple Touch is limited to 16 shades of gray.

Magazines and newspapers are in the Library of the NOOK Color and the NOOK Simple Touch; on the NOOK Color they will also appear on the Daily Shelf.

To buy a single issue of a periodical

An individual copy of a magazine or newspaper will stay on your NOOK or in your B&N account for as long as you'd like.

Do this:

1. **Tap the cover.**

   The details page opens.

2. **Tap the Buy Current Issue button.**

3. **Tap Confirm.**

4. **Tap the Read button to open the magazine or newspaper.**

Figure 4-3: Tap the box with a price to start buying. Shown here is the screen on a NOOK Simple Touch with GlowLight.

Most magazines and newspapers offer free 14-day trials. Your credit card isn't charged if you cancel the subscription before the end of the trial. See Figure 4-4. To cancel a periodical subscription, go to your account at B&N, log in, and go to the Manage Subscriptions section.

Subscribe to a periodical

Follow these steps to subscribe:

1. **Tap the cover for the publication.**

   The details page opens.

2. **Tap the Free Trial button.**

3. **Tap Confirm.**

4. **Tap the Start My Free Trial button to confirm your order.**

Paying the bill

In most cases, anything you buy is charged to the credit card that's on record with Barnes & Noble. This book's bonus chapter online tells you how to update credit card information: www.dummies.com/go/nookereadersfdpe

Keep these things in mind:

- *Before* you go to the NOOK store, visit www.BN.com and make sure the balance on that card is associated with your account; when in doubt, call Barnes & Noble customer service for assistance.

- If you have a balance on your gift card, it's charged first. Anything left over is applied to your credit card.

- You can't accidentally buy a second copy of an eBook you already bought *for the account you are using with your NOOK.* If you have more than one account, you don't have this protection.

- You can pre-order eBooks if you have a billing address in the U.S., the U.K., and in other countries where the growing NOOK system expands in coming years. I discuss traveling internationally with a NOOK in Chapter 7. When the eBook is officially published, your credit card is charged and the book is downloaded to your NOOK.

- Connect to the NOOK store to have new periodical issues and pre-ordered (and now published) eBooks downloaded to your NOOK.

Figure 4-4: Most magazines and newspapers offer single copies as well as subscriptions, and many allow a trial subscription that can be canceled without charge.

> ✔ If you subscribe to a periodical, your credit card is billed on the 15th calendar day after the purchase. After that you're billed monthly. For example, if you start a free trial on January 5, your first charge is on January 20 and, after then, on the 20th of each month. See Figure 4-5.
>
> ✔ You can cancel a subscription at any time and get a prorated credit. Visit www.BN.com to cancel the subscription.

Writing a WishList

I have lots of wish lists: 72-inch 3D plasma TVs, suitcases full of professional digital cameras, and a new car to replace my flivver the next time it gets muddy. You know, the essentials of life. I also used to keep a list of books I want to read. Instead, now I add to my electronic WishList.

Your WishList lives on your NOOK. The WishList shows the title, cover, price, and the date you add it to the list. Your WishList can include books, magazines, and newspapers; the NOOK Color version can also include apps.

Add something to your WishList

Do this:

1. **Go to the B&N store.**

2. **Tap the book or periodical cover.**

   The details page opens.

3. **Tap the check box beside WishList.**

   The title is added.

Review your WishList

Do this to review the WishList on your NOOK Color:

1. **Tap the My Account button in the upper right corner of the store.**

2. **Tap My WishList.**

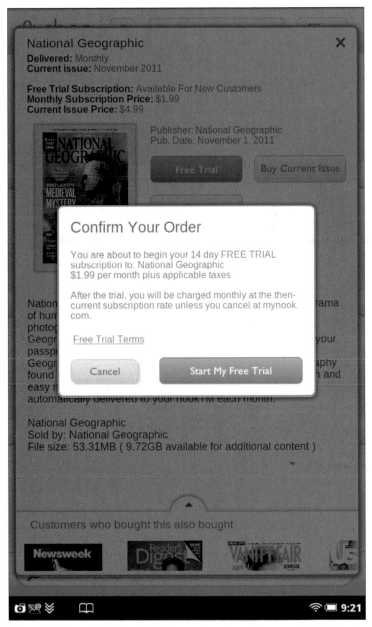

Figure 4-5: Free trials of periodicals can be ordered from your NOOK, but can only be canceled by visiting the NOOK Store website.

Do this on the NOOK Simple Touch:

1. **Tap Shop.**

   You're taken to the store's home page.

2. **Tap Popular Lists.**

3. **Tap the WishList link.**

   To buy an item on your WishList, tap the price button next to the item's name.

4. **Tap the Confirm button.**

Archiving Books or Periodicals

Your NOOK may eventually run out of storage space. When that happens, it's time to place them in the archives.

A book that you archive *isn't* gone forever. It's just not on your NOOK anymore. You can download it to your eReader again. See Figure 4-6. On both devices, you need an active Wi-Fi connection to the Internet to archive or recall an archived item.

Archiving from the NOOK Color

Here's how to put a book or periodical into deep storage:

1. **In the Library, press and hold on the cover for a book, magazine, or newspaper.**

2. **Tap Archive.**

   The NOOK Color tells the NOOK store what you want and the item moves to a section called Archived in your Library.

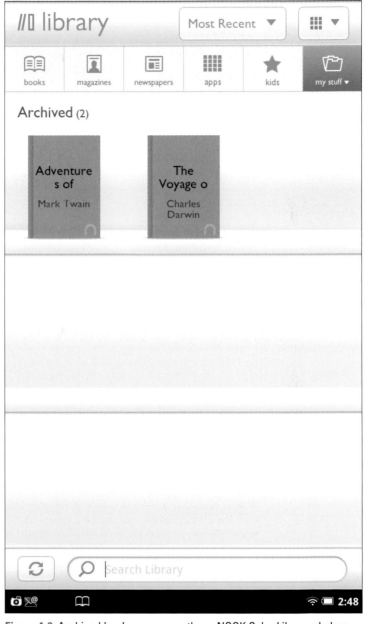

Figure 4-6: Archived books appear on these NOOK Color Library shelves, but you must reconnect to the NOOK store to retrieve the files if you want to read them.

Archiving from the NOOK Simple Touch

Here's how to archive a book from the NOOK Simple Touch:

1. **Tap the cover of a book or periodical you want to archive.**

   The reading material will open.

2. **Tap anywhere in the text.**

   The reading tools open.

3. **Tap More.**

4. **Tap Archive.**

   A dialog box asks you to confirm your intentions.

5. **Tap Confirm.**

   The book moves to the Archived section.

Unarchiving from the NOOK Color

Do this to bring back something you've archived:

1. **In the Library, tap My Stuff.**

2. **Tap My Shelves.**

3. **Scroll through the shelves to find the Archived section.**

4. **Press and hold on the cover of what you want to retrieve.**

5. **Tap Unarchive.**

   The book is sent to your NOOK Color and now you can read it.

Unarchiving from the NOOK Simple Touch

Do this to bring back something you've archived:

1. **In the Library, tap the arrow.**

2. **Tap Archived.**

   You'll see titles that have been put into deep storage.

3. **Tap what you want to retrieve.**

4. **Tap the Unarchive button next to its title.**

   The book comes back to your NOOK Simple Touch now you can read it. If it doesn't appear within a minute or two, tap the Sync button at the top of the Library screen to update your Library.

Getting in Sync

You can update, or *sync,* your NOOK Color or NOOK Simple Touch to your B&N account.

Syncing does this:

- ✔ Updates all of your currently purchased content (except archived material).

- ✔ Lets you know of any updates, LendMe offers, and other notices.

You don't have to worry about keeping track of what is where. B&N does that for you.

Syncing is the same on both the NOOK Color and NOOK Simple Touch, but the Sync icon is in different spots on each. See Figure 4-7.

Figure 4-7: In the Library, tapping the Sync symbol will update your collection via Wi-Fi. NOOK Color has the Sync icon in the lower left.

To perform a sync, do this:

1. **Make sure your Wi-Fi is on and connected to the Internet.**

   You should see the Wi-Fi symbol in the status bar if you're connected. If you don't, see Chapter 5 for instructions.

2. **Go to the Library.**

3. **Tap Sync, the icon with two curved arrows forming a circle.**

   On the NOOK Color, the Sync button is in the lower left corner. On the NOOK Simple Touch, the icon is in the upper right.

Shopping Securely

Let me to ask a few questions:

- ✔ Will you ever loan your NOOK to someone else?

- ✔ Will family members, friends, acquaintances, or perfect strangers ever have access to your NOOK when you're not around?

- ✔ Can you conceive the possibility that your NOOK might someday (perish the thought) be lost or stolen?

If the answer to any of these questions is Yes or Maybe, make it more complex to buy something: Add a password. Make it a pretty good one, too. This is different from requiring a passcode just to unlock the NOOK for use.

The best password is one that is so complex and unobvious that no one can guess it. My favorite password is a phone number or address that has no direct connection to you but that you can recall from memory. Oh, and don't write it down on a sticky note applied to the bottom of the NOOK.

To set up your NOOK to require a password for purchases, see Chapter 1. It explains how to set up a password requirement and how to take one off.

Lending and Borrowing Books

You can loan most of your eBooks — just once — to another person who has a NOOK or a NOOK app. Look for a LendMe badge on a book cover to see if it's eligible. Figure 4-8 shows some potential lenders.

Courtesy of Barnes & Noble

Figure 4-8: On this NOOK Color, you can see the NOOK Friends who have books that you can ask to borrow.

Some conditions apply to the LendMe program:

- ✔ You can only lend from your registered NOOK to users of other registered B&N devices or apps.

- ✔ You can only loan books that you buy from Barnes & Noble.

- ✔ You can only lend one book at a time.

- ✔ You can lend an eBook just once, and for no more than 14 days. A user can return the book any time during the loan. If not, it's automatically returned at the end of 14 days.

- ✔ An offer to lend lasts seven days.

✔ While you loan out an eBook, you can't read it on your own NOOK.

✔ You can offer to lend a book to any e-mail address, but to accept the offer the recipient must have an e-mail address associated with a Barnes & Noble online account.

✔ You can lend a book from anywhere that has Wi-Fi.

✔ You can't lend a book that you're borrowing.

✔ You can't save a copy of a book that you're borrowing.

If you're borrowing a book, a colored bar on its cover tells you how many days remain on the loan. When the loan is over, the cover will be fade; if you tap the cover, you can buy it from the Barnes & Noble store.

Lending a book

To lend a book from your Library, follow the steps according to which NOOK model you have.

Do this:

1. **Press the ⋂ button.**

    The reading tools open.

2. **Tap Library.**

3. **Press and hold on a book's cover.**

4. **Tap LendMe.**

5. **Tap the choice that fits the way you want to notify someone of the LendMe offer.**

    • Email: Choose a contact. If you haven't entered any contacts or linked your account, select Contacts and tap the Add Contact button to type an e-mail address for the recipient.

    • Facebook wall. You must have linked your NOOK to that account.

    • Google Gmail. You must have linked your NOOK to that account.

Borrowing a book

You can borrow a book from anyone who has a B&N account; get in touch with the Contacts or Social pages and request a title. To find out which of your contacts have lendable books, start the LendMe application. The process is slightly different on the NOOK Color and Nook Simple Touch.

Chapter 3 tells how you can make your lendable books private.

Borrowing from a NOOK Friend on the NOOK Color

Start the NOOK Friends application by doing this:

1. **Press the ∩ button.**

    The quick nav bar opens.

2. **Tap Apps.**

3. **Tap the Nook Friends app.**

4. **Tap the LendMe button at the top of the screen.**

5. **Tap in the search box at the bottom of the screen.**

6. **Type a title or author.**

7. **Tap Look Up.**

8. **Tap Borrow beside the book you want.**

Now you need to request the loan. Here's how:

1. **Press the ∩ button.**

    The quick nav bar opens.

2. **Tap Settings.**

3. **Tap Social.**

4. **Tap the Manage My NOOK Friends.**

    You see your list of NOOK Friends.

5. **Tap the Request button beside the name of a NOOK Friend who has the book you want.**

    A dialog box opens.

6. **Type a message.**

   Can I suggest you include the word *please* in your note?

7. **Tap Send.**

Borrowing from a NOOK Friend on the NOOK Simple Touch

To find out if any of your NOOK Friends has a book you want to borrow, you'll need to start the Manage My NOOK Friends app from the Social settings screen. Here's how:

1. **Press the ∩ button.**

   The quick nav bar opens.

2. **Tap Settings.**

3. **Tap Social.**

4. **Tap the right arrow beside Manage My NOOK Friends.**

5. **Tap the name of any NOOK Friend to see her lendable books.**

   If they have LendMe books available, you can ask to borrow one. Tap Request next to a book that's available for loan; you can also add a note to your friend, perhaps including a "please" and "thank you."

Managing Your Library

The Library is where all documents live on your NOOK. You can look at everything all at once or browse through categories. The NOOK Color and NOOK Simple Touch are very similar but not identical in their sorting of items.

To display your Library, press the ∩ button to show the quick nav bar and then tap Library. (You guessed this, right?)

Knowing your categories

NOOK Color and NOOK Simple Touch have these categories in common:

- ✔ **Books.** The NOOK's raison d'être!

- ✔ **LendMe.** Books you're borrowing, those you've borrowed, those offered, those you've loaned, and those you can loan. You'll also see a button that starts the LendMe app.

- ✔ **Archived.** Books or periodicals that you've removed from your NOOK; get the files back at the B&N store. This category doesn't show if you haven't archived any files.

NOOK Color Library categories

In addition to Books, LendMe, and Archived, the NOOK Color has these categories:

- ✔ **Magazines.** Periodicals you bought from the NOOK store or received by subscription through the store.

- ✔ **Newspapers.** Newspapers you bought from the NOOK store or that arrive by subscription.

- ✔ **Apps.** *Applications* (aka *apps*) are small programs. These are the ones you've downloaded from the NOOK Store.

- ✔ **Kids.** Books for children, including NOOK Kids picture books (some with interactive features, audio, and video), magazines, and apps purchased from the NOOK Store.

- ✔ **My Stuff.** Other content, including files you've side-loaded from a personal computer to your NOOK Color:

    - • **My Shelves.** Shelves you made yourself.

    - • **My Files.** Personal document files.

         If a microSD memory card is in your NOOK, you'll be able to switch between files stored on the NOOK itself and the card.

- ✔ **Everything Else.** Well, not quite everything, but certain things that don't fit elsewhere, like NOOK study titles. This category appears only if you have files that don't fit on a different shelf.

- ✔ **Archived.** Books and periodicals you've archived.

NOOK Simple Touch Library categories

To get to the shelves of the NOOK Simple Touch, tap the Category Menu in the upper left corner of the Library screen:

- ✔ **All.** Yes, everything in the Library, without categorization.

- ✔ **Newsstand.** Magazines or newspapers you've bought from the NOOK store. If you haven't bought a periodical, you won't see this category.

- ✔ **Shelves.** If you've made your own shelves to organize reading material, they will appear under this heading. See the following section for how to do that.

- ✔ **My Files.** Files including PDFs, or EPUB eBooks you got for free.

If a microSD memory card is in your NOOK, you'll be able to switch between files stored on the NOOK itself and the card.

Building your own shelves

You can add nearly unlimited shelves on your NOOK. See Figure 4-9.

Creating a shelf

You can create any shelf you want and call it anything that makes sense to you.

To create a shelf on your NOOK COLOR, do this:

1. **Press the ∩ button.**

   The quick nav bar opens.

2. **Tap Library.**

3. **Tap My Stuff.**

4. **Tap My Shelves.**

5. **Tap Create New Shelf.**

6. **Type a name for your shelf.**

7. **Tap Save.**

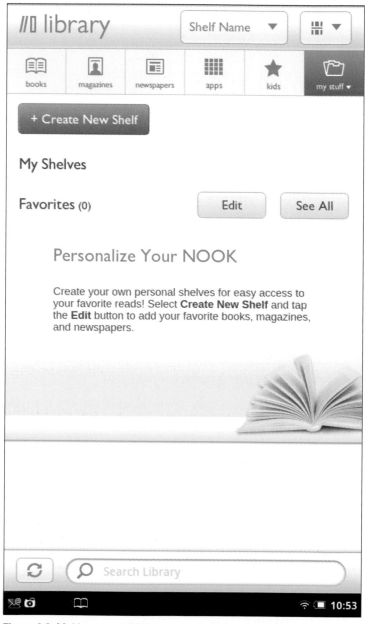

Figure 4-9: Making your NOOK your own includes the hammer-less process of creating shelves.

To create a shelf on your NOOK Simple Touch, do this:

1. **Press the ⋂ button.**

   The quick nav bar opens.

2. **Tap Library.**

3. **Tap Category.**

4. **Tap My Shelves.**

5. **Tap Add New Shelf.**

   A dialog box appears.

6. **Tap in the text field and type a name for the shelf.**

7. **Tap Save.**

You can rename a shelf:

1. **Tap the Edit button beside the shelf name.**

2. **Tap Rename.**

3. **Type the new name.**

4. **Tap Save.**

If you get rid of a shelf, your items are still in your Library. To get rid of a shelf, do this:

1. **Tap Edit beside the shelf you want to delete.**

2. **Tap Remove.**

   A dialog box asks if you're sure.

3. **Tap OK.**

 Sort your books and publications in just about any logical manner: by title or author (or most recent, for magazines). You can organize them different ways, too: in a grid, in horizontal shelves, or in a list.

Adding items to the shelf

After you build a shelf, you can move books and publications to it.

Do this to add items to a shelf:

1. **Tap the Edit button next to the shelf you're loading.**

   You'll see a list of your books and periodicals.

2. **Tap the check box beside the titles.**

   If something *has* a check mark, it will go on the shelf. If it *doesn't have* a check mark, it won't go on the shelf.

3. **Tap Save.**

Searching your NOOK

You can quickly burrow through all of the items in its memory. (And on the NOOK Color, you can search the Internet, too.)

To use it, do this:

1. **Tap the white quick nav arrow in the status bar.**

2. **Tap Search.**

3. **Type the author, title, or subject of what you're looking for.**

4. **Tap the magnifying glass icon.**

   If the NOOK Color doesn't find a result, it tries the B&N store (if you're currently connected to the Internet).

 Press the ∩ button and search from the quick nav bar; it's much more inclusive than looking in the Library. Tap any result to get more information about the item.

Telling a Book (or Mag) By Its Cover

To some extent, you *can* tell a book by its cover. A marker, or *badge,* on the cover can also tell you whether something's completely downloaded. (Tap the cover to resume downloading.)

Something for nothing

Here are some worthy sites to visit for great free reads from authors who no longer need the money:

✔ Project Gutenberg at www.gutenberg.org

✔ ManyBooks.net at www.manybooks.net

✔ FeedBooks at www.feedbooks.com

✔ Google Books at http://books.google.com

Here are the merit badges for content:

✔ **New.** Ready to be opened and read.

✔ **Sample.** A free sample.

✔ **Download.** Waiting to download from the Barnes & Noble website.

✔ **Pre-order.** A title that's for sale, but hasn't been released. If you buy, it'll arrive at the first opportune moment.

✔ **Recommended.** A NOOK Friend or contact endorses this read.

✔ **LendMe.** You can loan this to someone.

✔ **Lent.** You're borrowing this. The badge also tells the number of days remaining on the loan. (The owner can't read it when you're borrowing it.)

✔ **Returned.** On the NOOK Simple Touch, you've borrowed and sent back.

✔ **Google.** A Google eBook, which you can get for free on the web.

Buying from Stores Besides B&N

Just as there are other brands of eReaders on the market, there are other online bookstores. Google Play and Kobo sell eBooks, but you'll have to buy from your desktop or laptop computer, not from your NOOK. See Figure 4-10. Kobo sticks to books, magazines, and newspapers; as this book goes to press, they don't offer music, videos, or apps.

Amazon, one of the largest eBook sellers, uses its own file types for eBooks. Neither NOOK Color nor or NOOK Simple Touch can use the Amazon file type.

Figure 4-10: Google Play sells eBooks that you can download to your computer and then side-load to your NOOK.

Be ready with your NOOK and the USB cord. Here's how to buy an eBook from Google Play or Kobo:

1. **Using your desktop or laptop computer, visit** play. google.com.

   You don't have to type *http://www.*

2. **Create a free account.**

3. **Look for eBooks.**

   When you find an eBook you want to buy, choose the EPUB file if one is offered; a PDF file will work, but not as elegantly.

4. **When you find one you want to buy, click it.**

5. **Type in your credit card information.**

6. **The eBook is sent to your computer.**

   If the book file is protected by digital rights management (DRM), you'll need a software program like Adobe Digital Editions. I explain Adobe Digital Editions in Chapter 5.

7. **Side-load the file from your computer to your NOOK.**

   Chapter 5 has the directions for how to side-load.

Sony has its own eBookstore at http://ebookstore.sony.com. To use it you'll need to download the Sony Reader app to your desktop or laptop computer and use it to transfer files to the NOOK.

Filing That Under Non-Book

In addition to displaying books, magazines, and newspapers, you can use your NOOK to look at files created in lots of computer applications. You can only read the files. You can't edit or otherwise change them on your eReader.

These file types work with both NOOK eReaders:

- ✔ PDF (You can convert files to PDF format)
- ✔ EPUB

These kinds of files only work for the NOOK Color:

- ✔ Word: doc, docx, docm, dot, dotx, dotm
- ✔ Excel: xls, xlsx, xlsm, xlt, xltx, xltm
- ✔ PowerPoint: ppt, pptx, pptm, pps, ppsx, ppsm, pot, potx, potm
- ✔ Plain Text: txt
- ✔ HyperText Markup Language: htm, html, xhtml

Always keep backup copies of important files on your personal computer. As wondrous as it is, your NOOK could break or be stolen or misplaced.

If you want your NOOK Color or NOOK Simple Touch to display files that you make on a desktop or laptop computer, use a full-featured word processor or graphics application (for example, Microsoft Word and Adobe PhotoShop or Adobe PhotoShop Elements).

Converting files on a computer

The NOOK Simple Touch can display files only if they're in EPUB or PDF format.

To save a file from Word as a PDF, do this:

1. **Open the file in the program on your laptop or personal computer**

2. **Click Save As.**

3. **Choose PDF.**

If you're offered a choice between standard and minimum sizes for the file, choose Minimum if you only want to read the file on the NOOK Color. If you're going to print the file from your computer, choose Standard.

Converting photos and drawings

You can use a graphic program made by Adobe (or another company) to prepare photographs or images that you can display on your NOOK Color in its photo gallery, or as a wallpaper for the home page. Chapter 1 tells how to choose a wallpaper.

You can also side-load images onto the NOOK Simple Touch, although they're only shown in gray when the device is in sleep mode; I'm not going to disagree if that sounds like a large investment of time for a small return, although it is a nice custom touch.

There are many ways to prepare image files for the NOOK, but here is one sequence:

1. **Open the graphic program on your computer.**

2. **Choose Save As and rename the copy.**

That way you don't lose the original higher resolution and larger file.

3. **Resize the photo or drawing.**

   For the NOOK Color, that's about 4 inches by 6 inches. For the NOOK Simple Touch, that's about 3.5 inches by 5 inches.

4. **Convert the image to 72 or 96dpi.**

   Either resolution is fine.

5. **NOOK Simple Touch: Change the image to grayscale.**

6. **Convert the file to a compressed JPG file.**

7. **Side-load the file(s) from the computer to the NOOK.**

   See Chapter 5 for details of side-loading.

8. **Choose a folder depending on your NOOK model:**

   - NOOK Color: My Files
   - NOOK Simple Touch: Wallpaper folder

Chapter 5

Doing Tougher Stuff: Wireless, Side-Loading, Adding, Updating

. . . .

In This Chapter

▶ Going wireless with a NOOK

▶ Side-loading books and other files

▶ Organizing folders

. . . .

*B*uying something to read on your NOOK requires a Wi-Fi link to the Internet. Go another step and link your reading to friends. Finally, you can use the NOOK Color to browse the web and use e-mail. Alas, the NOOK Simple Touch doesn't work as a web browser. I discuss using the web and e-mail on the NOOK Color in Chapter 6.

Working the Net Without a Wire

The NOOK Color and the NOOK Simple Touch have a Wi-Fi receiver and transmitter, which connects your eReader to a wireless router that plugs into a standard Internet connection. Boom — you're online. See Figure 5-1.

Courtesy of Barnes & Noble

Figure 5-1: The NOOK Color's web browser can do almost everything that a personal computer's web browser can. Shown here is the popular YouTube site.

You don't have to connect via Wi-Fi to read eBooks or periodicals on your NOOK Color or NOOK Simple Touch. You *do* need Wi-Fi to load reading materials to your NOOK.

Wi-Fi systems are all around us. Here are the most common types:

- ✓ **Home.** I am assuming you've already set up your own Wi-Fi router at home and connected it to a wired cable modem or DSL phone modem.

- ✓ **Office or organization:** An office, library, or school, for example.

- ✓ **Open system.** Coffee shops, stores, and some local governments have created free (open) Wi-Fi.

- ✓ **Pay sites.** Some locations (including airports) sell access to the Internet.

To save battery power, turn off the Wi-Fi system any time you don't need it. Press the ∩ button, tap Settings, tap Wireless, and slide the Wi-Fi button to the Off position.

Connecting to Wi-Fi on a NOOK

Your NOOK will automatically ask if you want to connect to a Wi-Fi network if you walk into a Barnes & Noble store. It will also ask if you want to reconnect to a Wi-Fi network you've previously worked with. See Figure 5-2.

The following information is shown for the networks:

- ✓ The name of the network.

- ✓ The strength of the signal. The more dark, stacked lines you see, the stronger the signal. A strong signal generally means things will be faster and more reliable.

- ✓ Whether the signal is open or locked. A lock symbol means you need a password. If you don't know the password, ask the home owner or barista.

Here's how to connect to a Wi-Fi network:

1. **Tap the network's name.**

   If the network is locked or secured, a dialog box will appear. Tap inside the box and type the password.

2. **Tap Connect.**

You may be asked to create an account with a username and password, or asked to enter a password (or *key*).

You may be asked to enter your credit card information (to buy time online). Read the terms carefully before you give a credit card number or other information. If you're paying to use the Wi-Fi, you'll see terms and conditions that you must accept if you want to go onto the web. A pay or commercial site usually calls for the automatic display of a web page on your NOOK's browser; fill in the details there.

Network
name

Locked
system

Signal
strength

Figure 5-2: The Wi-Fi settings screen on the NOOK Color shows networks detected by the device and some basic information about them.

Some "free" networks (at coffee shops and the like) give their customers the password when you buy something (like a cup of coffee); some hotels may offer free service only to registered guests. You may see terms and conditions, a login screen, and a credit card information request. The NOOK Color will detect this sort of network, but you will need to fill in details on a page that will open in the web browser on your NOOK.

To connect to an open or unsecured network, just tap the network's name.

Side-Loading Files to the NOOK

So: You've got an eBook on your desktop computer and you want to put it on your NOOK Color or NOOK Simple Touch. You need to *side-load*. I don't know why it isn't called *transferring*. Perhaps it's part of a plot to remind us that we're still in the thrall of computer geeks.

 You can also your NOOK to store backup copies of files you might need. For example, if you're heading out on a trip to make a presentation or to share family photos, store files on the NOOK. If you need to get the files, just attach the NOOK to a desktop or laptop computer and side-load them.

Have your USB cable ready. You know, the one that came with your NOOK. This is the same cable you use to recharge your battery (without the AC adapter). See Figure 5-3.

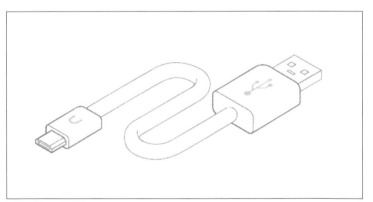

Courtesy of Barnes & Noble

Figure 5-3: Both NOOK Color and Simple Touch come with a USB cable that connects to a computer. The small end attaches to the eReader and the larger to a USB port on the computer.

 The very small end of the USB cable plugs into the port on your NOOK. The larger end attaches to a USB port on any current computer. At either end, *never* try to force a plug into place. The cable should attach easily; if at first you don't succeed, turn the cable over and try it that way.

Playing Manhattan Transfer

To side-load files from your personal computer to your NOOK
Color or NOOK Simple Touch, do this:

1. **Turn on your NOOK and a Windows or Mac personal
   computer.**

   Make sure your NOOK isn't in sleep mode.

2. **Connect the smaller end of the USB cable that came
   with your NOOK to your NOOK.**

3. **Connect the larger end of the USB cable to a USB
   port on your personal computer.**

   If the computer asks if you want to install a driver for
   a NOOK device, click Cancel. After you're connected,
   your computer should say it has detected a new disk
   drive. The drive may be called MYNOOK, NOOK, or
   Media.

4. **On your computer, double-click the detected drive.**

   You'll see folders.

5. **Click and drag personal files to the My Files folder.**

   When you move files from one device to another, the
   originals are copied to the new spot. If you have a
   microSD memory card in your NOOK, books, magazines,
   or newspapers that you side-loaded are listed under
   My Files.

6. **Eject your NOOK.**

   When you're done moving files, you're supposed to
   eject or *unmount* the NOOK from your desktop or
   laptop computer. The way you do this depends on
   your operating system. For details, see the section
   in this chapter called "Ejecting the NOOK from a
   computer."

7. **Disconnect the USB cable.**

   The NOOK will say it's processing the files.

You can move files from your NOOK to your computer (for
archive or backup).

Organizing folders

Within the My Files folder, you can sort files into these secondary or subfolders.

NOOK Color or NOOK Simple Touch:

- ✔ **Books.** This one you can figure out, right?
- ✔ **Documents.** The NOOK Color can display (but not edit) these types of files:

  - PDF
  - EPUB
  - Word: doc, docx, dot, dotx, or dotm
  - Excel: xls, xlsx, xlsm, xlt, xltx, or xltm
  - PowerPoint: ppt, pptx, pptm, ppx, ppsx, ppsm, pot, potx, or potm
  - Plain text: txt
  - HTML: htm, html, or xhtml
  - Comic book archive: cbz

  The NOOK Simple Touch can use PDF or EPUB files.
- ✔ **Magazines.** Any periodicals other than newspapers.
- ✔ **Newspapers.** Keep your stacks neatly piled here.

NOOK Color only:

- ✔ **Music.** Put audio files here. The NOOK Color can play MP3, WAV, aac, amr, mid, midi, m4a, and ogg formats.
- ✔ **Photos.** Put JPG and other image files here.
- ✔ **Videos.** The NOOK Color can play videos as large as 2GB in Adobe Flash, 3gp, 3g2, mkv, mp4, or m4v formats. You can't watch a lengthy movie or TV show.
- ✔ **Wallpapers.** These images are specifically intended for display in the background of the Home Page.

NOOK Simple Touch only:

- ✔ **Screensavers.** Digital photographs to be used as a screensaver.

Use only the USB cable provided with your NOOK Color or NOOK Simple Touch, or an exact duplicate. There are many different types of USB cables and using the wrong one could damage the physical connector on the NOOK Color and possibly cause problems to the reader's electronics.

Moving files from internal memory to a microSD card

If you have a microSD or microSDHC memory card installed in the slot of your reader, when you tap My Files you'll see a button labeled Memory Card in the Library.

To copy files from the internal memory of your NOOK Color or NOOK Simple Touch to its microSD memory card, do this:

1. **Turn on your NOOK and your computer.**

2. **Connect the USB cable to your NOOK and to your desktop or laptop computer.**

   The small end of the USB cable goes into your NOOK. The larger end goes into a USB port on your computer. *Don't* force a plug into place.

3. **Transfer the files from the NOOK to a folder on the computer.**

4. **Move the same files from the computer back to the My Files folder on the NOOK.**

5. **Eject or unmount the NOOK from the computer.**

   For details, see the section in this chapter called "Ejecting the NOOK from a computer."

   To move files the other direction, from the memory card to the internal memory of the NOOK, follow the same instructions but move from My Files to the My NOOK or NOOK folder on the eReader.

Using Adobe Digital Editions

If an eBook or periodical is protected with digital rights management (DRM), the NOOK can't display it without proper permission being granted. If you get a current copyrighted EPUB or PDF from a bookseller other than Barnes & Noble, you'll probably have to use something to grant that permission. The same process may apply if you borrow books from a library.

The most popular rights-management programs is Adobe Digital Editions (ADE), which is offered free to users by Adobe Software. ADE side-loads and authorizes files under have DRM. Adobe Digital Editions lets you have only six copies of a particular book. See Figure 5-4.

Library view icon

Figure 5-4: Adobe Digital Editions goes on a computer and handles the transfer and digital rights management for protected files.

 Some libraries use OverDrive software to handle eBook lending. Read the instructions provided by the library for how to get and use OverDrive. In most instances, OverDrive is provided free to card-carrying patrons of libraries that use it.

Getting a copy of Adobe Digital Editions

If you don't have a copy of Adobe Digital Editions on your desktop or laptop computer, you'll need to create an Adobe ID and then download the software.

From the computer, do this:

1. Turn on your computer.

2. **In the web browser, go to** `www.adobe.com/products/digitaleditions`.

3. **Click Download Now.**

4. **Follow the instructions to put it on your computer.**

Authorizing a book using Adobe Digital Editions

Using your desktop or laptop computer, go to Google Play or the Kobo store or another other online bookseller. Then follow these steps:

1. **Buy and download the EPUB (preferred) or the PDF version of the eBook.**

   The store will send an ACSM (Adobe Content Server Manager) file to your computer.

2. **Find the ACSM file on your computer.**

   It may be on the desktop or in a folder associated with the bookseller.

3. **Click the ACSM file.**

   It should open in the Adobe Digital Editions program. If the file doesn't open on a Windows computer, right-click the file. Click Open with Menu and then click Open with Adobe Digital Editions.

   The eBook should now appear in the All Items shelf in the library view of Adobe Digital Editions (on the right).

4. **If you aren't in library view, click the icon in the upper left of Adobe Digital Editions.**

5. **Turn on your NOOK and connect it to the small end of the USB cable.**

6. **Connect the larger end of the USB cable to a USB port on your computer.**

   Adobe Digital Editions will tell you that it has recognized your NOOK; it should appear as a device under Bookshelves on the left side of your computer screen.

7. **If the NOOK isn't recognized, close Adobe Digital Editions and reopen it with the already NOOK on and the USB cable plugged in.**

8. **Click and drag the eBook from the right pane onto the NOOK icon in the left pane.**

   If you can't drag the book onto the NOOK icon, the eReader isn't properly authorized to the software and your Adobe account. Check out the ADE help screens for how to authorize the hardware.

9. **After a few seconds, click the NOOK icon and find the eBook under the eReader folder.**

10. **Eject the NOOK from your Windows computer (or unmount it from your Mac computer).**

    For details, see the section in this chapter called "Getting ejected."

    The NOOK will say that it's processing the file(s).

11. **When that's done, press the ∩ button on your NOOK.**

    The reading tools open.

12. **Tap Library.**

13. **Look in My Files for the file you have side-loaded to the eReader.**

    Open it by tapping its cover. If you put the files in a new folder that you created, or in a folder other than My Files, go to that location to find it.

Reactivating Adobe Digital Editions on your NOOK

You may have to reactivate Adobe Digital Editions on your eReader from time to time; actions by other programs may remove records of authorizations given to hardware. The process is to deactivate the program and then reactivate.

Here's how:

1. **Start Adobe Digital Editions running on your computer.**

2. **Deactivate the software:**

   • On a Windows machine, press Ctrl+Shift+D.

   • On a Mac computer, press Cmd+Shift+D.

   Press all three keys at the same time.

3. **Deactivate the hardware:**

   - On a Windows machine, press Ctrl+Shift+E.

   - On a Mac computer, press Cmd+Shift+E.

   The Device Deactivation dialog box opens.

4. **Find and click your NOOK eReader.**

5. **Click Deactivate.**

6. **Unplug one end of the USB cable from your NOOK, wait two seconds or so, and then reinstall the plug.**

   The program should display the Device Authorization dialog box.

7. **Enter the same Adobe ID you used previously.**

Loading the right Calibre

Calibre is a free program you can download and install on your personal computer (Windows, Mac, or Linux) and use to *convert* (change) a wide range of file formats into EPUB or PDF formats.

It converts these formats:

   ✔ RTF

   ✔ PDF

   ✔ TXT

It makes these files into EPUB or PDF formats that your NOOK can use. See Figure 5-5. You can get a copy by visiting the web at http://calibre-ebook.com.

Getting ejected

When you connect your NOOK Color or NOOK Simple Touch to a computer, ejecting the eReader before unplugging the USB cable can help you avoid damaging the copied files. (This is sometimes also referred to as *unmounting* the device.)

You can eject the NOOK by clicking an Eject button (displayed onscreen in some desktop applications), or you can follow the directions given here.

Figure 5-5: Calibre converts many file formats into EPUB or PDF form.

Ejecting the NOOK from Microsoft Windows-based computers

Do this:

1. **Open the My Computer (or Computer) folder.**

2. **Click the icon for the NOOK.**

   Don't double-click. You just want to highlight the icon.

3. **Right-click the NOOK icon.**

4. **Click Eject.**

5. **Unplug the USB cable from the computer.**

   You can also unplug the cable from the eReader or leave it attached.

   After the reader is ejected and the USB cable removed from the computer, the NOOK will tell you that it's processing new files. Give it a moment to put books and documents on the shelf.

Ejecting the NOOK from Apple-based computers

Do this:

1. **Open the Finder and select the NOOK.**

2. **Click File.**

3. **Click Eject NOOK.**

   If you also have a microSD card installed in your eReader, eject that memory card as well. Chapter 2 explains how to install and format a microSD or microSDHC card.

4. **Unplug the USB cable from the computer.**

   You can also unplug the cable from the eReader or leave it plugged in.

Chapter 6

Going Online, Grabbing Mail, and Getting 'Appy with NOOK Color

*T*he NOOK Simple Touch offers access to the NOOK Store and social networks. The NOOK Color goes several steps beyond. It can go online with a web browser, send and receive e-mail, display full-color photos and (short) videos, and play music. The NOOK Color also can use apps that extend its capabilities.

Browsing the Web on Your NOOK Color

The NOOK Color can browse the Internet fairly fast and show websites that have streaming media such as movies, news, and music. See Figure 6-1.

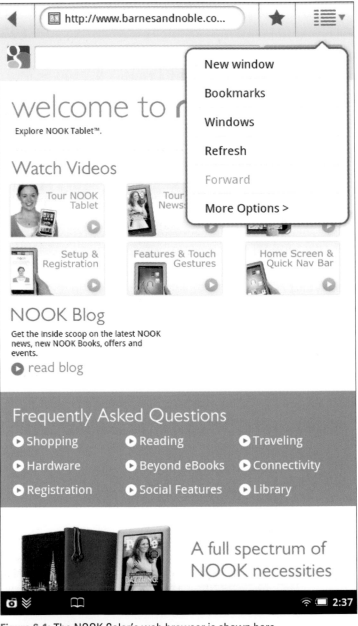

Figure 6-1: The NOOK Color's web browser is shown here.

It's a pretty amazing offering for a device that's mainly an eReader. However, don't confuse this with a full-featured web browser on a high-power laptop or desktop computer; the little processor within the NOOK Color isn't in that class. It will get you where you want to go, but not always as quickly. And some website features won't work properly or look very good on the eReader's relatively tiny screen. Think of it this way: The NOOK Color is an eReader that also can surf the web, rather than a full-featured computer that can also be used to read eBooks.

To open the web browser, do this:

1. **Make sure your NOOK Color is connected to a Wi-Fi network and signed in (if necessary).**

   Look for the Wi-Fi icon in the status bar. If it isn't there, tap Settings. Then tap Wireless and turn on the radio.

2. **Tap the white arrow in the status bar.**

   The quick nav bar opens.

3. **Tap Web.**

   If the Web button is grayed out and says Disabled, well, the browser's been disabled or turned off. To enable or disable the web browser, see the following section.

The NOOK Color web browser will be familiar if you've used a browser on a personal computer. The features include the following, and they're labeled in Figure 6-1:

 ✔ **Address bar.** Displays the web address (technically the URL or Uniform Resource Locator, but almost no one outside of the propeller-head labs call it that anymore) for the current page.

   To visit a different page,

   1. **Tap in the address bar.**

   2. **Type an URL or tap one of the options that comes up.**

   3. **Tap Go.**

 ✔ **Search Google.** Not surprisingly for a browser that's part developed by the Internet search engine giant Google, you can tap a button to jump directly to the Google page and search. See Figure 6-2.

words. Word origins not only shed light on their current meaning, but offer clues to their ...

Obsolete Word of the Day: **battologist** [·↑]
obsoleteword.blogspot.com/2007/08/**battologist**.html

Aug 28, 2007 – **battologist**. This is someone who repeats the same thing for no reason. It comes from the Greek word for stammerer. posted by the scribbler ...

Battologist - definition of **Battologist** by the Free Online Dictionary ... [·↑]
www.thefreedictionary.com/**Battologist**

Legal dictionary. Financial dictionary. Acronyms. Idioms. Encyclopedia. Wikipedia encyclopedia ? **Battologist**. 0.01 sec. Bat`tol´o`gist. n. 1. One who battologizes. ...

battologist - Encyclopedia [·↑]
www.encyclo.co.uk/define/**battologist**

battologist - Meaning and definition. ... Look up: **battologist**. **Battologist** Bat·tol'o· gist noun One who battologizes. Found on http:// www.encyclo.co.uk/webster/B/23 ...

Battologist...Are You One? | | CF Web ProfessionalsCF Web Professionals [·↑]
www.cfwebprofessionals.com/blog/general/**battologist**-are-you-one/

Oct 30, 2010 – I was surfing the web this morning, for now I can't remember what – when I ran into the word: **battologist**. It piqued my interest. ...

the **battologist** - YouTube [·↑]

www.youtube.com/watch?v=hVnW3lSeb2Q

Aug 10, 2010 - 8 min - Uploaded by violettemaschine
Our annual entry into the 48 Hour Film Project-Denver! This was the first year I was director of ...

More videos for **battologist** »

battologist's Music Profile – Users at Last.fm [·↑]
www.last.fm/user/**battologist**

⊠@ 📷 ≫   📖   📶 ▭ 4:36

Figure 6-2: It's easy to jump out of almost any page, or from the web browser itself, to the Google search engine. Behold my "battologist" search results.

✔ **Back button.** Tapping the left-facing arrow takes you to the page or address you most recently visited.

✔ **Bookmarks.** Also referred to as *favorites*. Tapping the star lets you set favorite sites as bookmarks. Tap the thumbnail for the page you want to visit.

✔ **Options menu.** Tapping the down-facing arrow (at the far right of the address bar) opens a menu with these options:

> • **New window.** You can open more windows to quickly move from one page to another while leaving a previous one still available. Multiple windows running animations or video will slow down the browser and the eReader itself.
>
> • **Bookmarks.** Jump to pages you have bookmarked.
>
> • **Windows.** Names of pages you're looking at right then.
>
> • **Refresh.** You can redisplay updates or changes to a web page.
>
> • **Forward.** Go to a page you've seen in the same visit.
>
> • **More Options.** Add a bookmark, search for a word or phrase on the current page, display page info, see downloads, or jump to the browser's Settings menu.

Working with bookmarks

Making and managing bookmarks is an important skill.

Bookmarking a web page

To establish a bookmark for the current Web page using a pop-up menu, do this:

1. **Press and hold anywhere on the page, except for sections that are active (like links or fields).**

   A good choice is usually a blank piece of the screen.

2. **Tap Bookmark This Page.**

   A dialog box opens.

3. **Tap in the Name field and type a name for the bookmark.**

4. **Accept the Web address (URL) for the current location.**

   That is, unless you want to name it something else.

5. **Tap OK.**

Visiting a bookmarked page

The purpose of having bookmarks is to give you fast access to the pages. Here's how to use your bookmarks:

1. **Tap the star icon at the top of the browser.**

   A window will show *thumbnails* (small images) of bookmarked pages. You can change the display by tapping List View.

2. **Tap the thumbnail or address for the page you want.**

Deleting a bookmarked page

Too many bookmarks defeat the purpose of shortcuts; you'll waste a lot of time trying to find the one you want. It's worth weeding them out from time to time.

Do this to delete a web page bookmark:

1. **Tap the Options menu.**

   The Options menu has a down-facing arrow and is on the far right beside the address bar.

2. **Tap Bookmarks.**

3. **Press and hold on the thumbnail for the bookmark you want to delete.**

4. **Tap Delete Bookmark.**

   Are you sure?

5. **Tap OK to confirm.**

Changing text size in the browser

The NOOK Color browser can use different size text. You've got Normal and, going down, there's Small and then Tiny. If Normal isn't big enough, there's Large and then Huge. Choosing larger text will make words easier to read, but you'll have to drag to see all of the information on a page. See Figure 6-3.

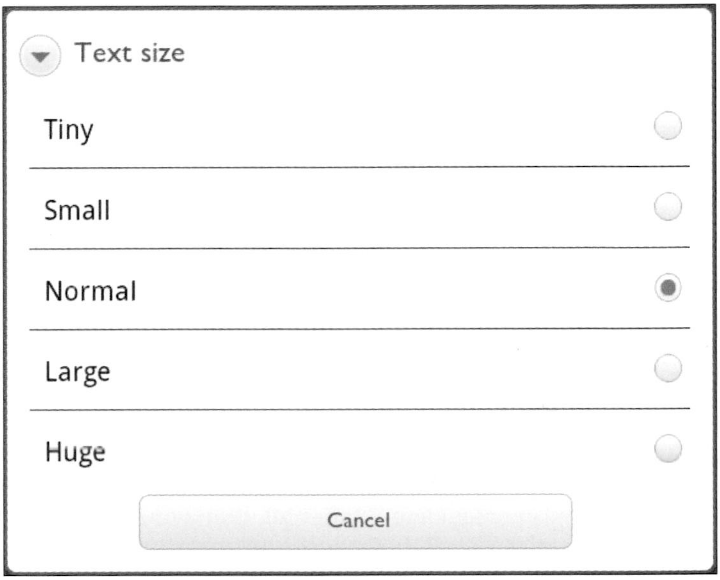

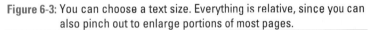

Figure 6-3: You can choose a text size. Everything is relative, since you can also pinch out to enlarge portions of most pages.

To change the text size, do this:

1. **Tap the Options menu.**

   The Options menu has a down-facing arrow and is on the far right beside the address bar.

2. **Tap More Options.**

3. **Tap Settings.**

4. **Tap Text Size.**

5. **Tap the text size you want to see in the browser.**

6. **Tap OK to confirm your choice.**

Zooming in or out on a web page

You can zoom in and out on an entire web page. On some pages that makes more sense than enlarging the text type; experiment to find which works best at particular addresses.

 ✔ To **zoom in,** tap twice quickly on the portion you want to be at the center of the enlarged section. Once you have zoomed in, you can swipe left, right, up, or down to move around on the page.

 ✔ Tap the (+) in the lower left to zoom in further.

 ✔ To **zoom out,** tap twice or tap the magnifying glass with a minus sign (–).

Setting the browser's home page

The web browser has a pre-set home page.

When you first use your NOOK Color, the web browser home page is a Barnes & Noble site devoted to all things NOOK Color. You're almost certainly going to return to the B&N web page at some time — after all, that's one of the main places to buy new eBooks. I suggest bookmarking the B&N web page for easy access.

But consider changing your home page to something that makes broader use of the wonders of the web. You can start anywhere: a search engine like Google or Bing, a news page like *The New York Times,* an online shopping site, the mother ship for this book series at www.dummies.com, or perhaps my humble site at www.sandlerbooks.com (where you can send me a message from the Contact page). See Figure 6-4.

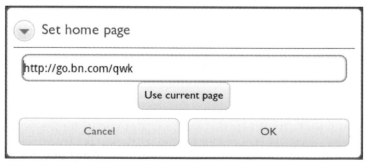

Figure 6-4: The page you choose as home is always displayed first when you start the browser.

Do this to change your home page:

1. **Tap the Options menu.**

2. **Tap More Options.**

   The Options menu closes and a new pop-up menu opens.

3. **Tap Settings.**

   The Settings screen opens.

4. **Tap Set Home Page.**

5. **Tap Use Current Page to use what you see as your home page.**

   Or, type the address (URL) for the page you want to assign as your home page.

6. **Click OK.**

Disabling or re-enabling the web browser

Your NOOK Color, your web browser. That is, unless someone else uses your eReader.

You can disable the web browser temporarily.

Someone who's using the NOOK Color with a disabled browser can still access the Library and the B&N store; buy books, magazines, newspapers, and apps (although you can require entry of a credit card and a NOOK password); send and receive e-mail, and share recommendations by e-mail, Facebook, Twitter, or Google.

Disabling the web browser

To be able to disable (and later re-enable) the web browser, you have to first set up a restriction passcode. This keeps other people from disabling or enabling the browser without your permission.

If you expect other people to use your eReader, it's wise to set a restrictions passcode even if you have no intention of disabling the browser.

Here's how to disable the web browser:

1. **Press the ∩ button.**

   The quick nav bar opens.

2. **Tap Settings.**

3. **Tap Security.**

   The Security screen opens.

4. **Tap Restrictions.**

   A numeric keypad opens.

5. **Type a four-digit passcode.**

   That passcode will be required to be entered any time you want to disable or re-enable the browser.

6. **Type the code again.**

   The Restriction menu will appear and you'll have the opportunity to limit the web browser by tapping in the right box. You can also restrict social apps.

Re-enabling the web browser

If you use a restriction passcode, you have to enter that code any time you want to return to the Restrictions menu.

Here's how to re-enable the web browser:

1. **Press the ∩ button.**

   The quick nav bar opens.

2. **Tap Settings.**

3. **Tap Security.**

   The Security screen opens.

4. **Tap Restrictions.**

5. **Type the four-digit passcode.**

6. **Tap in the box next to Browser.**

What number should you use as a restriction passcode? Any number that's tough to guess. I suggest the last four digits of a phone number that *isn't* yours and isn't obviously associated with you. How about the last four digits of an old phone number no longer in use? Or the last four digits of a pizza parlor you frequent?

The restrictions passcode is a separate secret code from the device lock passcode that you can also set for the eReader. The device lock code is required any time the NOOK Color is turned *on.*

Setting web privacy and security

There are people out there who know if you've been sleeping and know when you're awake. What's more, they know if you've been bad or good. For goodness' sake — or at least for your own confidentiality — pay attention to your NOOK Color's web browser privacy settings (as well as on any computer or phone-based browser you use).

The NOOK Color does offer a reasonable number of privacy and security tools, but I'm not willing to promise that this eReader (or any other) is absolutely safe from unwanted intrusion. See Figure 6-5.

A clever snoop may be able to get some of your personal information. Be careful about the sort of information you store on your eReader and what you send using the Wi-Fi connection.

   ✔ First line of defense: Use tough passwords on any accounts you visit.

   ✔ Second line of defense: Pay attention to the privacy settings on the NOOK Color and clear out personal information on a regular basis. The following sections tell you how to do that.

✔ Third line of defense: Don't leave open any doors through which a snoop might enter. For example, don't be obvious: taping a note to your tablet with passwords, using your significant other's name as a password, and that sort of thing. Hundreds of thousands of people use PASSWORD as their password; yes, really.

Although they're closely related, the browser on the NOOK Color distinguishes between protections of privacy and security. Privacy settings are to help protect the story of where you've visited on the Internet and the information you've given to online forms and menus.

Controls for both privacy and security settings are on the same menu page. Here's how to reach them:

1. **Tap the Options menu in the web browser.**

   The Options menu has a down-facing arrow and is on the far right beside the address bar.

2. **Tap More Options.**

3. **Tap Settings.**

4. **Tap Clear Cache to put a check mark in the box.**

   The cache stores some pages, images, and other downloaded content. Tapping Clear Cache erases that until the next time you visit pages.

5. **Tap Clear History to put a check mark in the box.**

   History records the URLs you've visit.

6. **Tap Accept Cookies to *get rid of* the check mark in the box.**

   A *cookie* is information sent to you by pages you visit; your browser accepts cookies unless you turn off that option. Some websites don't let you visit if you don't accept cookies; that's a tradeoff you have to judge for yourself.

7. **Tap Clear All Cookies to put a check mark in the box.**

   All the cookies on your NOOK Color are deleted. Doing this *doesn't* tell the browser *not* to accept future offerings, but it does clear the stuff that has accumulated.

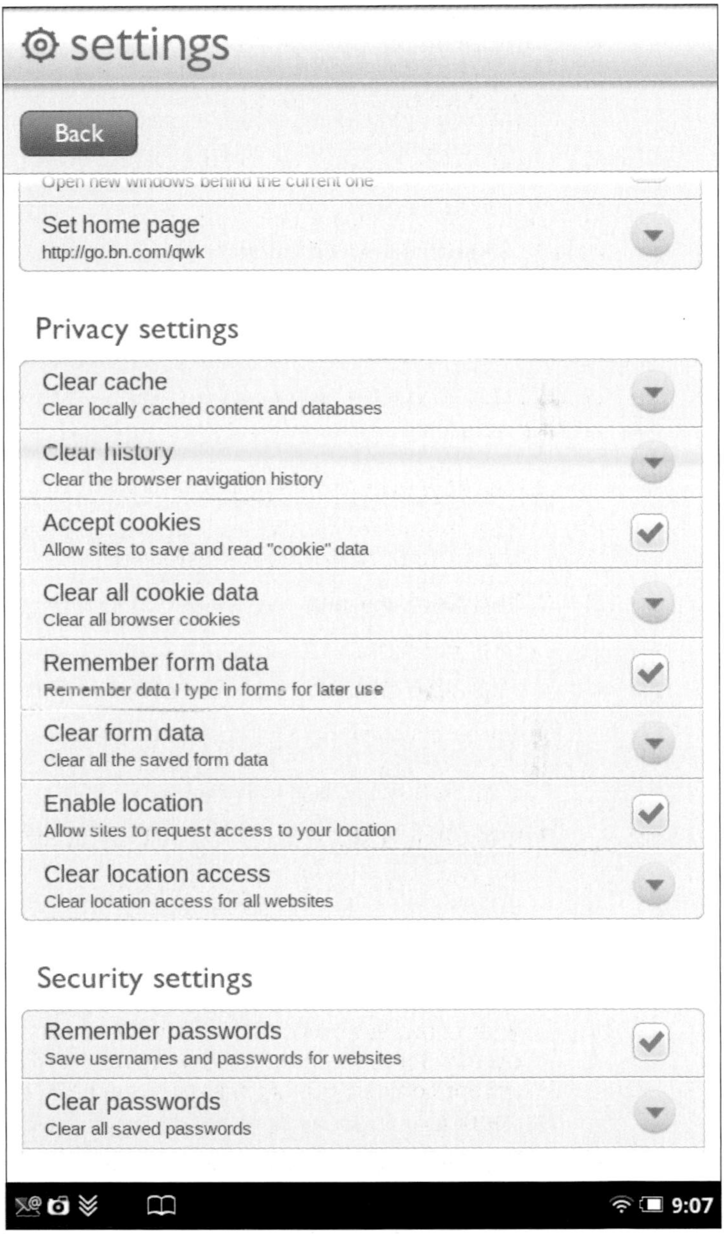

⚙ settings

Back

Open new windows behind the current one

Set home page
http://go.bn.com/qwk

Privacy settings

Clear cache
Clear locally cached content and databases

Clear history
Clear the browser navigation history

Accept cookies
Allow sites to save and read "cookie" data

Clear all cookie data
Clear all browser cookies

Remember form data
Remember data I type in forms for later use

Clear form data
Clear all the saved form data

Enable location
Allow sites to request access to your location

Clear location access
Clear location access for all websites

Security settings

Remember passwords
Save usernames and passwords for websites

Clear passwords
Clear all saved passwords

9:07

Figure 6-5: The NOOK browser offers reasonable privacy and security
settings.

8. Tap Remember Form Data to *get rid of* the check mark in the box.

When you fill out a form that asks for common information (name, address, phone number, and e-mail address, for example), the browser can automatically fill in the info on new pages that ask for the same data.

Some information, such as bank accounts and credit cards may also be stored. The Remember Form Data option is turned on until you turn it off.

9. Tap Clear Form Data to put a check mark in the box.

You must turn off this feature of your NOOK will record new data until the next time you clear this portion of memory.

10. Decide whether you want to turn on Enable Location.

This feature lets websites know your general whereabouts. That can mean localized ads and discounts for your city when you're online. That isn't always a bad thing.

11. Tap Clear Location Access to put a check mark in the box.

Tapping here will remove information about general places you've signed on to the Internet.

12. Decide whether you need to turn off Remember Passwords.

Remember Passwords is on unless you turn it off. If you leave it on, the browser will save usernames and passwords for web sites. If you do any banking or buying online, you run the risk of someone stealing information from your NOOK Color. It's better to tap Remember Passwords and clear the check mark in that case.

13. Tap Clear Passwords to put a check mark in the box.

Turning on Clear Passwords gets rid of password information from the browser. If you keep Remember Passwords turned on (see Step 12), the browser will add any future passwords to its memory.

14. **Decide whether you want to turn on Show Security Warnings.**

    The browser will warn you if it sees a problem with a website's security. If you turn off this feature, you won't see warnings.

 The NOOK Color browser is set up to block *pop-up windows;* those are the ads or notices that appear over certain web pages — mostly to the annoyance of users. However, you may need to see a pop-up that's related to a site. You can turn the block on or off from the Page Content Settings of the web configuration options.

Carrying the E-Mail

The NOOK Color has a basic Email app that lets you send and receive messages from one or more e-mail accounts, including Gmail, Yahoo!, and Hotmail. Barnes & Noble doesn't provide e-mail service of its own. (Alas, there's no e-mail on the NOOK Simple Touch.)

The NOOK Color inbox will retrieve the 25 most recent messages from each account linked to your NOOK, sorted by date and time received. The e-mails can have attachments, but displays only those that are in one of the format recognized by the NOOK Color. See Figure 6-6.

Starting the Email app

The Email application is in the Apps window. Here's how to open it:

1. **Press the ∩ button**

   The quick nav bar opens.

2. **Tap Apps.**

3. **Tap Email.**

If you've already set up an e-mail account on your NOOK Color, you'll see your inbox. If you haven't linked an account to the NOOK, you'll see a dialog box that helps you do that.

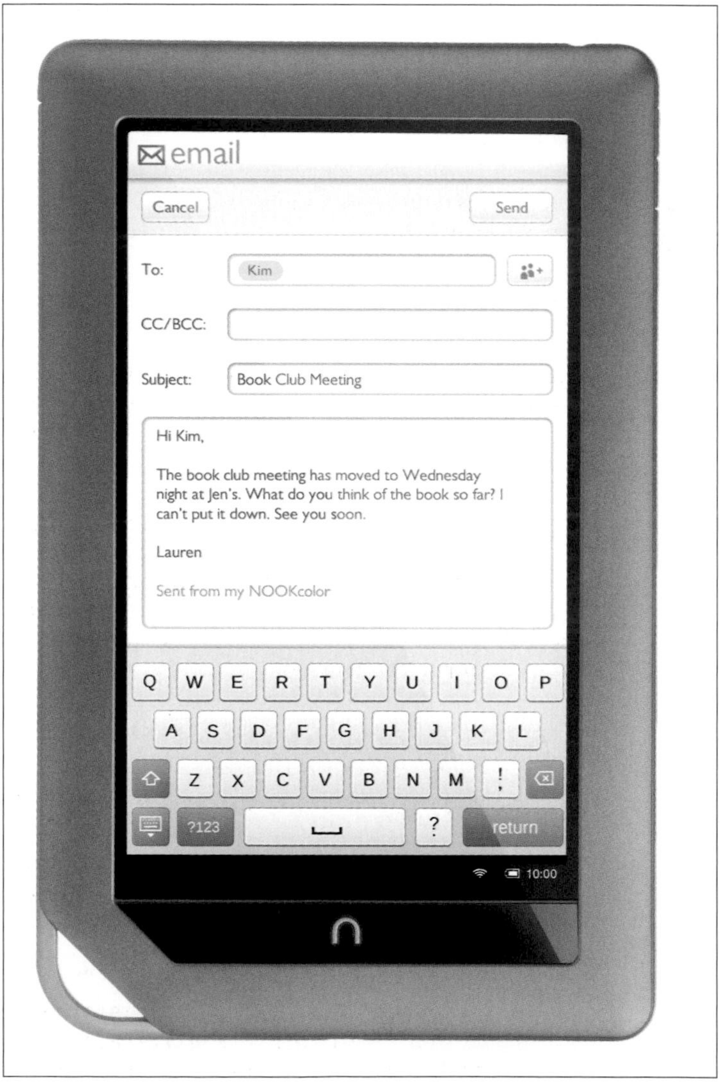

Courtesy of Barnes & Noble

Figure 6-6: The NOOK Color can be used as a portable extension of your desktop e-mail device.

All business

The NOOK app can't help with your corporate e-mail, calendar, or contact sync. However, you can buy the TouchDown app through the NOOK store to add support for accounts based on Microsoft Exchange Server systems. For more details, you can visit `www.nook color.com/email`.

Your NOOK must be connected to a Wi-Fi network to send and receive mail.

Managing e-mail accounts

If you set up different e-mail accounts, you'll have to choose one as your default account. The account you choose is the one that sends messages from your NOOK Color (unless you manually select a different account).

You can associate an existing e-mail account with the app on your NOOK Color: automatic or manual. The automatic process works well for most web-based e-mail services like Gmail or Hotmail; go ahead and use it if you can. You may have to go manual if your e-mail company has some non-standard or higher security barriers.

Setting up an e-mail account using automatic configuration

Here's how to use the automatic configuration:

1. **When the NOOK displays the e-mail account setup screen, type the e-mail address for the account you want to use.**

2. **Type the password for that account.**

   The NOOK ordinarily hides the password as you enter it; if you want to see it as you enter it, tap to place a check mark in the Show Password box.

3. **Tap to place a check mark beside Send E-Mail from This Account By Default.**

Only do this if this is the account from which e-mail messages should come.

4. Tap Next.

The NOOK will try to connect to the e-mail account and set up a connection using standard settings. If it is successful, you will see a new screen with two fields.

- **Account name.** Tap here and type a name for this account. For example, you might want to call it *Janice's Hotmail.* The name doesn't appear on messages you send.

- **Your name.** What you type here appears on outgoing messages as the sender. Recipients will see it in the From field.

5. Click Done to finish.

Setting up an e-mail account using manual configuration

If for some reason the automatic configuration doesn't work, try these steps.

Here's how to manually link an e-mail account to your NOOK Color:

1. Gather information about your account, including the name of your account's e-mail server.

The server might be something like IMAP.*mycompany server*.com or POP.*yourcompany*.com. Get this information by using a web browser to visit the support pages for your e-mail provider company or by calling their help desk.

Or, check the settings in your computer-based e-mail app. For example, in a Microsoft app provided to Windows users, click Tools, click Accounts, and then highlight an account. Next, click Properties. In the dialog box, click Servers and other tabs.

2. Open the account setup screen on your NOOK.

You have a choice between automatic and manual.

3. Type the account's e-mail address.

4. **Type the password for that account.**

   The NOOK usually hides the password as you enter it; if you want to see it as you type it, tap a check mark in the Show Password box.

5. **Tap to place a check mark beside Send E-Mail from This Account By Default.**

   Only do this if this is the account from which e-mail messages should come.

6. **Tap Manual Setup.**

   The Server settings screen opens.

7. **Tap in the Domain Username field and type your username for the account.**

8. **Tap in the Server Name field and type the name of the server.**

9. **If your e-mail service requires SSL, tap to place a check mark next to Use Secure Connection (SSL).**

   SSL stands for Secure Sockets Layer.

10. **If your service requires you to accept SSL certificates, tap to place a check mark next to Accept All SSL Certificates.**

11. **Tap Next.**

    The NOOK tries to connect to the e-mail account and set up a connection. If it works, you'll see a new screen with two fields:

    - **Account name.** Tap here and type a name for this account. For example, you might want to call it *Janice's Hotmail.* The name doesn't appear on messages you send.

    - **Your name.** What you type here appears on outgoing messages as the sender. Recipients will see it in the From field.

12. **Click Done to finish.**

Adding an account

After you've set up at least one e-mail account for your NOOK Color, you can add others. On the Email screen, click the Add Account button. Follow the preceding steps for an automatic or manual configuration.

Reading e-mail from different accounts

You can read incoming messages from any one of the accounts you have linked to your NOOK, or you can have all incoming messages combined in a single inbox.

To switch from one account to another, do this:

1. **Tap the Account menu at the top of the e-mail screen.**

2. **Select an individual account.**

   To see all of your messages from all accounts, select Combined Inbox instead.

Deleting an account

You can remove an account from your NOOK Email app. That doesn't mean you've closed the e-mail account with the provider you use (Gmail, Hotmail, or others), but it does remove the settings you've made on the NOOK for the account.

Downloaded messages from the account are also deleted. Depending on the account, the original messages may still be on the server; that's the standard setting for IMAP accounts.

Do this to delete an e-mail account:

1. **On the main e-mail screen, find the account you want to delete. Tap to put a check mark in the box beside it.**

2. **Tap the Delete trash can icon in the upper right of the screen.**

   You're asked to confirm your decision.

3. **Tap OK.**

Adjusting e-mail settings

You can customize the way the Email app works or make changes to account settings by going to the e-mail configuration screen. Here's how to make changes:

1. **Press the ∩ button and tap Apps.**

2. **Tap the Email app.**

3. **Tap the Accounts menu.**

   You'll see all the accounts on the device.

4. **Tap the gear icon beside the account you want to adjust.**

   The e-mail configuration menu opens. The following sections explain configuration items.

General settings

The items here control how the e-mail account is displayed on your NOOK Color and how messages are identified on a recipient's device. Tap the down arrow beside the first four items to open a menu; that's where you can make a change.

✓ **Account name.** The name you have given the account for display on your NOOK device.

✓ **Your name.** The name as it will appear in the From field on any message you send to another person.

✓ **Signature.** This short message appears at the bottom of any e-mail message you send. The default signature is *Sent from my NOOK.* You can change it to whatever you choose. See Figure 6-7. Some people use the signature to advertise for themselves or their organization. Some people use the signature to let people know how and when to contact them.

✓ **E-mail check frequency.** Tell the NOOK how often to check for new messages.

✓ **Default account.** Choose an account as the default for sending messages.

Notification settings

If you tap in the E-mail Notifications box and place a check mark, the status bar will show you each time new e-mail arrives.

In general, you change server settings only if there's a change to the specifications of an e-mail account or if your e-mail provider tells you to adjust them.

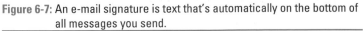

Figure 6-7: An e-mail signature is text that's automatically on the bottom of all messages you send.

Sending an e-mail

Sending an e-mail on the NOOK Color is straightforward for anyone who's done it on a computer. If you depend on your contacts list to find an address, use the NOOK's web browser instead of the Email app. Go online to your web-based e-mail service if it has its own linked contacts list.

Composing and sending an e-mail

Communicating via e-mail on your NOOK Color goes like this:

1. **Connect with Wi-Fi to the Internet.**
2. **Tap the Email app icon.**
3. **On the Email screen, tap the pencil icon in the upper left.**

   See Figure 6-8.
4. **Tap in the To field.**
5. **Type the address for recipients.**

   To send a message to multiple recipients, separate e-mail addresses with a comma.
6. **Tap in the Subject field and type a topic.**

   Include a subject for all your messages. Some antispam programs reject messages without subjects.
7. **Tap in the body of the message and type the e-mail.**

   The body is marked *Enter message here.*
8. **When you're finished, tap Send.**

Reading an e-mail

To read an e-mail received on your NOOK Color, tap its subject in the inbox. You might need to take a few advanced steps:

- ✓ To fully view a long message, tap the Get More button at the lower right.
- ✓ To see embedded images, tap the Show Pictures button.
- ✓ To open attachments, tap the View Attachments button.
  - • The attachments' names are listed.

- Tap an attachment's name to open it, if it is in a compatible format: PDF or Microsoft Office files will open for reading.

- Attachments (compatible or not) go in the My Files/Download folder.

Replying or forwarding messages

You can reply to a message or forward it to another person.

1. **Open the e-mail message.**

2. **Tap one of the following:**

   - **Reply.** Return a message to the original sender.

   - **Reply All.** Send a message to the original sender as well as all everyone else who received the original message.

   - **Forward.** Send the original message to someone else.

Moving or deleting messages

You can tidy up your NOOK Color without working up a sweat.

Here's how to move a message to a previously created folder in the Email app:

1. **Open a message.**

2. **Tap Move To (at the bottom of the screen).**

   A menu will show all available folders.

3. **Tap the folder where you want the message moved.**

Here's how to delete a message:

1. **Open a message.**

2. **Tap the Delete button at the bottom of the screen.**

If you want to delete more than one message at a time, go to the inbox to see the list of messages. Tap a check mark in the box beside messages you want to delete. Then tap the trash can icon at the upper right.

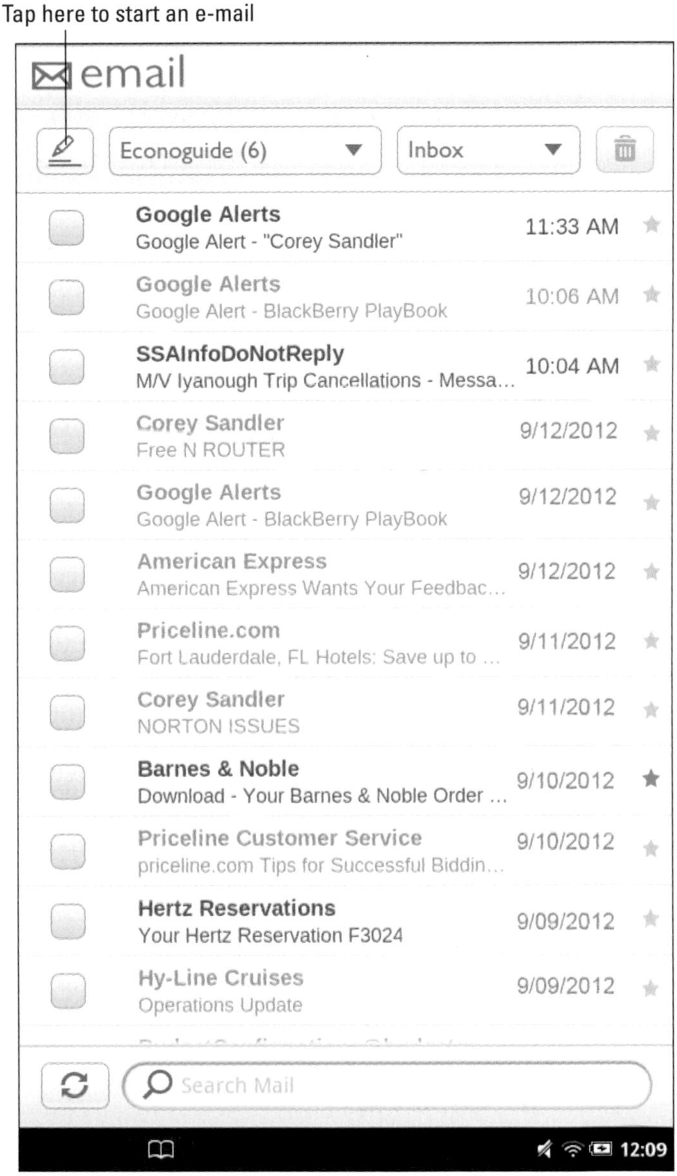

Tap here to start an e-mail

✉ email

| ✏ | Econoguide (6) ▼ | Inbox ▼ | 🗑 |

	Google Alerts	11:33 AM	☆
	Google Alert - "Corey Sandler"		
	Google Alerts	10:06 AM	☆
	Google Alert - BlackBerry PlayBook		
	SSAInfoDoNotReply	10:04 AM	☆
	M/V Iyanough Trip Cancellations - Messa...		
	Corey Sandler	9/12/2012	☆
	Free N ROUTER		
	Google Alerts	9/12/2012	☆
	Google Alert - BlackBerry PlayBook		
	American Express	9/12/2012	☆
	American Express Wants Your Feedbac...		
	Priceline.com	9/11/2012	☆
	Fort Lauderdale, FL Hotels: Save up to ...		
	Corey Sandler	9/11/2012	☆
	NORTON ISSUES		
	Barnes & Noble	9/10/2012	★
	Download - Your Barnes & Noble Order ...		
	Priceline Customer Service	9/10/2012	☆
	priceline.com Tips for Successful Biddin...		
	Hertz Reservations	9/09/2012	☆
	Your Hertz Reservation F3024		
	Hy-Line Cruises	9/09/2012	☆
	Operations Update		

| ⟳ | 🔍 Search Mail |

📖 🔇 📶 🔋 12:09

Figure 6-8: The Inbox lets you or search for, read, and delete messages.

Searching through e-mail

You can search through your e-mail for a name or content.

To lookey-loo, do this:

1. **From the e-mail inbox, tap in the Search field at the bottom of the screen.**

2. **Type the word or name you want to find.**

3. **Tap the Search button at the bottom right.**

   You'll see any e-mail that has the word, phrase, or name you asked to find.

4. **Tap a message to read it.**

App-lying Yourself on the NOOK Color

Applications, known as *apps,* are small programs. Barnes & Noble tries to make sure its NOOK apps focus on reading, but has allowed some carefully selected apps that move beyond bestsellers and classics.

Apps for the NOOK Color are sold through the NOOK store. See Figure 6-9.

Chapter 7 explains how you can root a NOOK Color. If you do that — it's tough for some users, but not impossible — you can gain access to most Android apps, not just B&N's.

Using the extras it came with

Your NOOK Color comes with Chess, Contacts, Crosswords, Music Player, My Media (to organize digital photos and videos), Pandora, and Sudoku. The following sections look at some of these extras.

To see the apps on your NOOK, press the ∩ button and tap Apps. To start an app, tap its icon in the Apps screen.

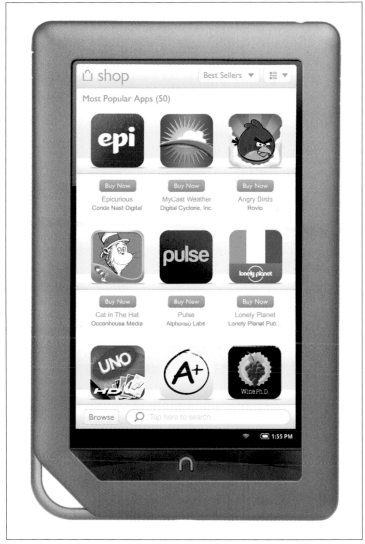

Courtesy of Barnes & Noble

Figure 6-9: The NOOK Store sells apps, but only NOOK Color and NOOK Tablet owners can download and install them.

Music Player

When you play music or audio, the sound comes from the small speaker on the back of the NOOK Color. It sounds better from headphones or earbuds plugged into the audio output jack on the eReader. See Figure 6-10. Chapter 5 tells you how to side-load.

These file formats will work on your NOOK Color:

- ✔ MIDI: mid, midi
- ✔ MPEG: mp3
- ✔ MPEG-4: m4a
- ✔ WAV: wav
- ✔ AAC: aac
- ✔ AMR: amr

Start the music player either by following either set of steps.

To play an audio file from the Library:

1. **Tap the My Files icon.**
2. **Tap the Music folder.**
3. **Tap the file you want to play.**

   The music player app will start.

To start the music player application directly:

1. **Press the ∩ button.**

   The quick nav bar opens.

2. **Tap the Extras icon.**
3. **Tap the Music icon.**

The music app has two modes: Browse and Now Playing. (A red band on the screen tells you which mode you're in; switch modes by tapping its icon in the upper right.) In Browse mode you can choose from the options in Table 6-1.

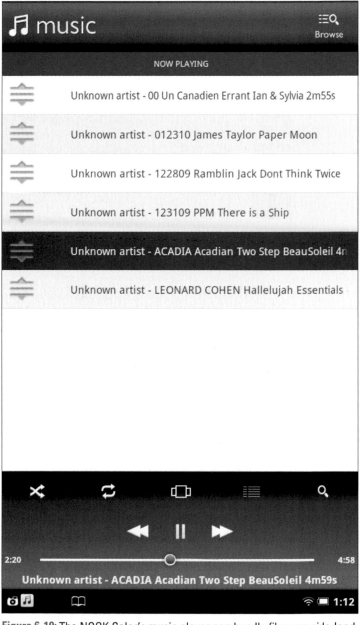

Figure 6-10: The NOOK Color's music player can handle files you side-load
from a personal computer or download from a web store.

Table 6-1   Browse Mode Options in the Music App

Icon	Option	What It Does
	Shuffle	Let the NOOK Color randomly play songs from your collection.
	Repeat	Tap once to repeat all your songs; tap tap twice to repeat the current song.
	Album art	Artwork for the song that's playing.
	Browse	See available songs.
	Search	Look for a title or artist.

When you're in Now Playing mode, you can press and hold on the gray arrow to the left of a song and drag the file up or down in the list to change the order of songs to be played.

To create a personal playlist, do this:

1. **Tap the list icon, which looks like musical notes.**

2. **Press and hold on a song title.**

3. **Tap Add to Playlist.**

4. **Tap New.**

5. **Type a name for the list in the dialog box.**

6. **Tap Save.**

You can move the songs around in a playlist, too: Tap the playlist, press on the gray arrow to the left of the song, and drag it where you want it. Tap Playlists to see all of them.

Photo Gallery

Though a picture may be worth a thousand words, it's hard to find nearly that many to describe the very basic photo display app that comes with the NOOK. See Figure 6-11.

First, remember that there's no camera in the NOOK Color. How do you get an image onto it?

 ✔ Side-loading them from a desktop or laptop computer (that you put there from a digital camera or the web). Chapter 5 explains how to side-load files.

 ✔ Saving them from websites you visit using the NOOK Color's browser.

 ✔ Saving them when they come as attachments to e-mails on the NOOK Color.

You can take a look at images two ways:

 ✔ Press the ∩ button and tap Apps. Tap Photo Gallery to see all the images (in small *thumbnail* versions) on your NOOK Color. Tap an image to enlarge it. You can watch a timed slideshow of all the images, if you prefer.

 ✔ Press the ∩ button and tap Library. Then tap My Files. If you have images in the Photos folder, you can go there and tap it. If you've made folders to better organize your images, using this route will let you go directly to them. For example, you might want to create (and fill with carefully selected photos) a folder called My Family Photos, and one called My Vacation Trip to Turkey, and so on.

A very basic photo editor is part of Photo Gallery. If you tap an image and make it full size, you can crop it, rotate it left or right, or use it as wallpaper. See Figure 6-12.

Figure 6-11: The Photo Gallery on the NOOK Color stores side-loaded images and videos, downloaded art, and built-in wallpaper.

Figure 6-12: The basic editor for the Photo Gallery allows cropping and rotation.

Pandora Internet Radio

I remember the days before radios were portable. We had our favorite radio stations, and we had our favorite DJs. But Pandora has opened another box. Think of it as a personal DJ who starts with a few songs or artists you like and then finds similar music. See Figure 6-13.

- ✔ When you first start Pandora on the NOOK Color, you're asked to create an account.

- ✔ You must be connected to Wi-Fi to listen to Pandora. If you're not sure, check the status bar for the Wi-Fi icon (pointed out in Figure 6-13).

- ✔ To play Pandora while you use the NOOK Color for other things, press the ∩ button or the quick nav bar to move to another activity.

- ✔ Tap the small P icon on the status bar to go back to the Pandora app.

- ✔ Create and fine-tune your own *stations.* You're allowed as many as 100.

Because of music licensing rights, Pandora is only available in the United States. The system will generally block access if you try to use the service from a Wi-Fi router out of the country.

Video Player

If you tap a video file, it will play it quite nicely on your NOOK Color — albeit this isn't a 100-inch plasma television with a surround-sound seven-channel audio system. The fact that the brightly lit screen is in your hand makes for a decent view of a small image.

The best quality video is either MP4 and M4V file format. The maximum file size that you can put on the NOOK Color is 2GB. NOOK Color works only with these video file types:

- ✔ 3GP

- ✔ 3G2

- ✔ MP4

- ✔ M4V

- ✔ OGG

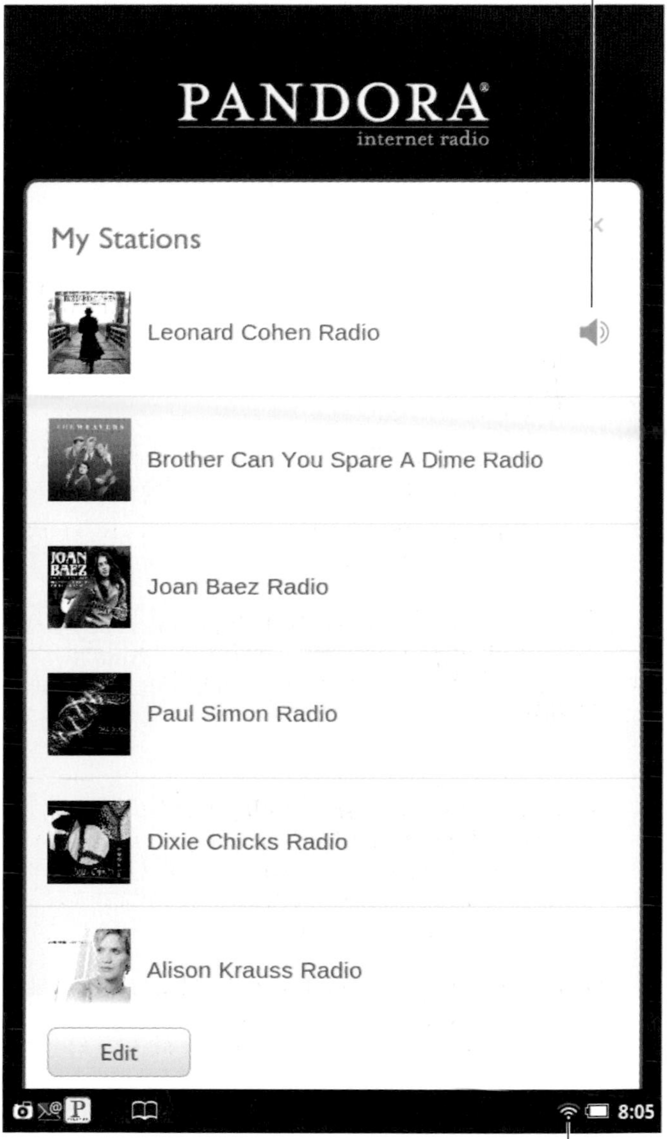

Now playing

Wi-Fi connection is made.

Figure 6-13: The stations you create further fine-tune the selections offered by Pandora.

Now, how do you get video files onto your NOOK Color?

✔ Side-load the files, which is explained in Chapter 5. Put the files in the Videos folder within My Files.

✔ Download a video directly from a website that sends the proper format. Choose a file that's for a smartphone or other mobile device and then click Download; it should arrive in your Downloads folder.

To play a video, do this:

1. **Press the ∩ button.**

2. **Tap Library.**

3. **Tap My Files.**

4. **Tap the Videos folder or the Downloads folder.**

5. **Tap the video you want to play.**

Adding apps from the NOOK store

Do you know any Angry Birds? Are you ready to have Words With Friends? Would you like to make your NOOK Color into a scaled-down Microsoft Office computer (a la Quickoffice Pro)? In these cases, and more, Barnes & Noble may have an app for that. See Figure 6-14.

Buying apps from the NOOK Store

The NOOK store is the official gateway to apps. Here's how to shop:

1. **Press the ∩ button**

   The quick nav bar opens.

2. **Tap Shop.**

3. **Tap Apps.**

4. **Browse around.**

   They're categorized, including bestsellers, new, utilities, games, education and reference, and more.

5. Tap an app's name, icon, or picture to read about it, including price.

Some apps are free, like banking online at your current bank. Some are supported by ads that you'll see.

6. Tap the Price button.

You're buying it now! Your linked credit or debit card is charged.

7. Tap Confirm.

The app starts downloading and installing on your NOOK Color. It can take several minutes to finish; if the process is interrupted, it automatically restarts when a wireless connection is restored. You can read more about an app if you press and hold its icon and then tap View Details.

You can get to apps in these places:

✐ Press the ⋂ button to show the home screen. Tap the Daily Shelf.

✐ Press the ⋂ button and tap Apps.

✐ Press the ⋂ button and tap Library.

Accepting a free trial version of an app

Some companies offer a free trial version of their app. A *free trial* isn't the same as a free app; the trial version is either time-limited (you'll be able to use it for a specific period of time or a specific number of uses) or has limited functions (you get all the features when you pay for the app).

Nevertheless, a free trial is a good way to try out an app. Look for a Free Trial button and tap it to download the sample.

Troubleshooting apps

If an app doesn't successfully get onto your NOOK Color, make sure you're connected to a working Wi-Fi signal.

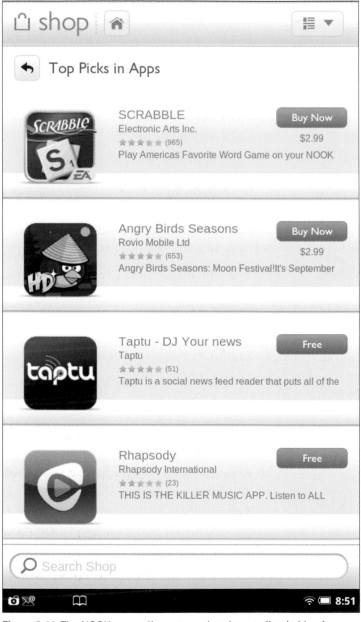

Figure 6-14: The NOOK store offers apps related to reading (with a few games and utilities thrown in).

You can start a download yourself:

1. **Tap the ∩ button.**

   The quick nav bar opens.

2. **Tap Apps.**

3. **Tap the app you want to download.**

   It should start to download and install. FYI: You can't side-load apps.

Here are some advanced troubleshooting steps:

1. **Press and hold the power button for about three seconds.**

2. **Tap Power Off.**

3. **Press the power button for three seconds.**

   It should turn on, and if you've set it up that way, you'll have to enter the passcode.

4. **Press the ∩ button.**

5. **Tap Apps.**

6. **Tap the app you want to fix.**

7. **Tap the Download button.**

And one more advanced procedure:

1. **Follow the preceding steps to display the troublesome app.**

2. **Press and hold on the app icon until a submenu appears.**

3. **Tap Archive.**

   The app is removed from your NOOK Color.

4. **Press the ∩ button.**

5. **Tap Library and tap the Archived shelf.**

6. **Press and hold on the icon for the app.**

   A submenu appears.

7. **Tap Unarchive to reinstall the app.**

Getting customer support for your app

Like it or not, Barnes & Noble passes your buck to the app makers when it comes to customer service issues. If you have a problem with an app, contact the company that made it.

You can find information about the developer two ways:

- ✔ Press and hold on the app's icon and then tap View Details.

- ✔ Press and hold on the app title on your NOOK Color. Tap Overview, and then tap Developer.

 If you accidentally buy the wrong app, run — do not walk — to a telephone and call Barnes & Noble customer service at 1-800-843-2665. They *may* be able to refund your fee, but only if they're notified immediately after the purchase.

Updating your apps

If an app that you bought gets updated, you'll see a notification in the lower left corner of the NOOK Color screen; tap it to get the newer version. You can also hunt for versions by tapping the Check for Updates button (in the upper right of the Apps section of your Library).

Archiving or deleting apps

If your NOOK Color runs out of space, you can archive apps. Archiving removes the app from your device, but lets you download and reinstall later. Chapter 3 tells you how to archive.

You can delete an app from your NOOK Color, but doing so permanently removes it from your device and from your B&N account and you can't take it (or get it) back.

To delete an app, do this:

1. **Tap Settings.**
2. **Tap Applications.**
3. **Tap an app.**
4. **Tap Delete.**

Chapter 7
Ten-Plus Tips and Tricks

In This Chapter

▶ Going about and abroad with a NOOK

▶ Viewing full websites on a NOOK Color

▶ Extending the NOOK warranty

▶ Resetting, deregistering, and wiping content

▶ Tuning in to a better Wi-Fi signal

▶ Shooting screenshots on a NOOK Color

▶ Rooting for rugged individualists

*I*n this chapter I try to anticipate as many of the possible problems as I can imagine. And I give you tips and tricks aimed at making the most of your NOOK, *plus* ways to help it live long and prosper.

Living with a NOOK

The NOOK is an electrical device. To keep it happy, you want to allow it to keep cool, dry, and avoid smashing it to pieces. Specifically:

✔ **Keep it dry.** Don't take the NOOK into the bathtub with you. I also suggest keeping cups of coffee and cans of soda as far away from your NOOK as possible.

✔ **Keep it at the right temperature.** If the temperature is too hot or too cold for you to function, get yourself and your NOOK to a more comfortable place.

✔ **Keep it in one piece.** NOOK devices are reasonably sturdy, but don't put it in your back pocket or use it as a stand for a potted plant.

Getting the Most from the Battery

Sometimes a perfectly fine NOOK plays dead. Okay, it's not *really* dead. But perhaps deeply asleep and unresponsive. Off and unwilling to turn on.

You can't replace the battery. If it fails during the standard one-year warranty, you'll have to send it in for repair.

A couple things can make a NOOK Color or NOOK Simple Touch appear dead even if it isn't. Here are the usual suspects:

✔ **The battery doesn't have enough power.** If your eReader starts acting squirrely, check the battery level in the status bar. It's along the top of the NOOK Simple Touch and across the bottom of the NOOK Color. A full battery means a full charge. Recharge the battery if need be. Chapter 1 tells you how.

✔ **Your recharger isn't getting juice.**

  • Make sure the recharger is plugged into a live outlet; don't use an outlet that's controlled by a wall switch.

  • If the charger is attached to a power strip, make sure it's on. You can test an outlet or strip by plugging a lamp into it.

  • Make sure the USB cable is properly and fully attached at each end. If the ∩ icon on the USB cable isn't glowing, it isn't charging.

I'm pretty good when it comes to technology, but I do have a confession: I once paid good money to a washing machine repair technician to learn that the water faucet was turned off. The same can happen with your battery recharger.

The battery will get warm as it's used. Warm — not egg-fryingly hot. If you think the internal battery is creating too much heat or is otherwise acting odd, turn off the NOOK and contact Barnes & Noble customer service at 1-800-843-2665.

Consider things you can do to make the battery last as long as possible:

- ✔ **Don't run the battery down to zero charge.** Turn off the NOOK when you see the low charge alert rather than letting it completely run out of juice. Recharge the battery fully before you use it again.

- ✔ **Avoid extremely high or low temperatures for use, recharging, or storage.** Don't leave your NOOK in the trunk of the car. Don't leave it on your desk in direct summer sunlight or near a heat register. And don't put it in the freezer with last night's leftover meatloaf.

- ✔ **Recharge the battery before a prolonged period on the shelf.** If you plan to put your NOOK away for a week or more, charge the battery to *at least* half full. And then turn it off completely by pressing and holding the power button for three seconds.

Barnes & Noble urges you to use only the AC adapter and the USB cable that came with your NOOK. If you need a second charger, they'll be happy to sell you one.

Turning Off, Tuning Out

Be sure to follow the instructions of flight attendants, doctors and nurses, and anyone else who has a real reason to ask you to turn off your NOOK.

If Wi-Fi is turned off, you can read eBooks and other publications, but you can't download anything, do any social networking (via Facebook or Twitter or Google), or use the web browser or the Email app (which only the NOOK Color has).

Turn off Wi-Fi this way:

1. **Press the ⋂ button.**
2. **Tap Settings**
3. **Tap Wireless.**
4. **Tap the Wi-Fi button to change it from On to Off.**

   Later, when you can turn it back on, tap again.

International NOOK of Mystery

Books are *intellectual property*. By that we mean that the ideas expressed within them have value and the form in which they are expressed is owned by either the author or the publisher. This is a good thing, because it helps authors and publishers put food on the table and keep the lights on.

But things get complicated when we deal with varying laws regarding copyright and licensing around the world. For that reason, NOOK eReaders can only be registered to a user who has a billing address in the U.S., its territories, or the U.K. B&N plans to add other international availability in coming months; check with customer service to track the expansion of the NOOK universe.

Once you have a NOOK and a properly registered account, here's what you can do anywhere in the world:

- ✔ Read anything that's already on your NOOK.

- ✔ Download already-purchased items where you can connect to a Wi-Fi system. There's a big *gotcha* in the middle of that sentence: You had to have bought the item while you were in the U.S., U.S. territories, or the U.K.; this includes orders, pre-orders, and subscriptions.

- ✔ You can lend or borrow books from NOOK Friends.

Oh, and one more thing: recharging. Your NOOK should hold on to its battery charge for a while. (The NOOK Simple Touch is usually good for a week or more of intensive reading, while the NOOK Color will run out after about four to six hours.)

The AC adapter that came with your NOOK won't plug directly into electrical systems in Europe, Africa, much of Asia, and some other places. In general, you'll need a plug adapter (not a voltage converter) to recharge when you're away from home.

You can recharge the NOOK Simple Touch by connecting its USB cable to the USB port of a laptop or desktop computer, but that computer must have a power source of its own.

Skipping Mobile Pages on NOOK Color

It's a fact: Your NOOK Color has a much smaller screen than a desktop or laptop computer does. For that reason, some websites are scaled-down version of their full pages. When you get your NOOK Color, it's set up to request these *mobile pages* when they're available.

But there is a solution, which involves sending a special User Agent request to websites:

1. **In the NOOK web browser, tap Settings.**
2. **Tap Page Content Settings.**
3. **Tap the down arrow beside Browser Mode. See Figure 7-1.**
4. **Tap in the circle beside an option:**

   - **Tablet Browser Mode:** This default setting uses mobile pages when available.

   - **Desktop Browser Mode:** This asks the browser to request a standard web page.

Getting Touchy-Feely

You're going to touch the screen. The NOOK Color and NOOK Simple touch are, after all, touchscreen devices.

↙ Try to keep your hands clean; don't eat a greasy pizza and then swipe your fingers across the screen. Clean up first.

↙ If the screen gets dirty, tap X to turn it off and clean it gently. Use a *slightly* damp soft cloth or the kind of cloth you use to clean eyeglasses. Don't use any chemicals to clean the screen; use a tiny dash of water on the cloth.

Consider buying a little house for your NOOK: A carrying case or sleeve protects the screen and keeps dust and minor spills out of the innards.

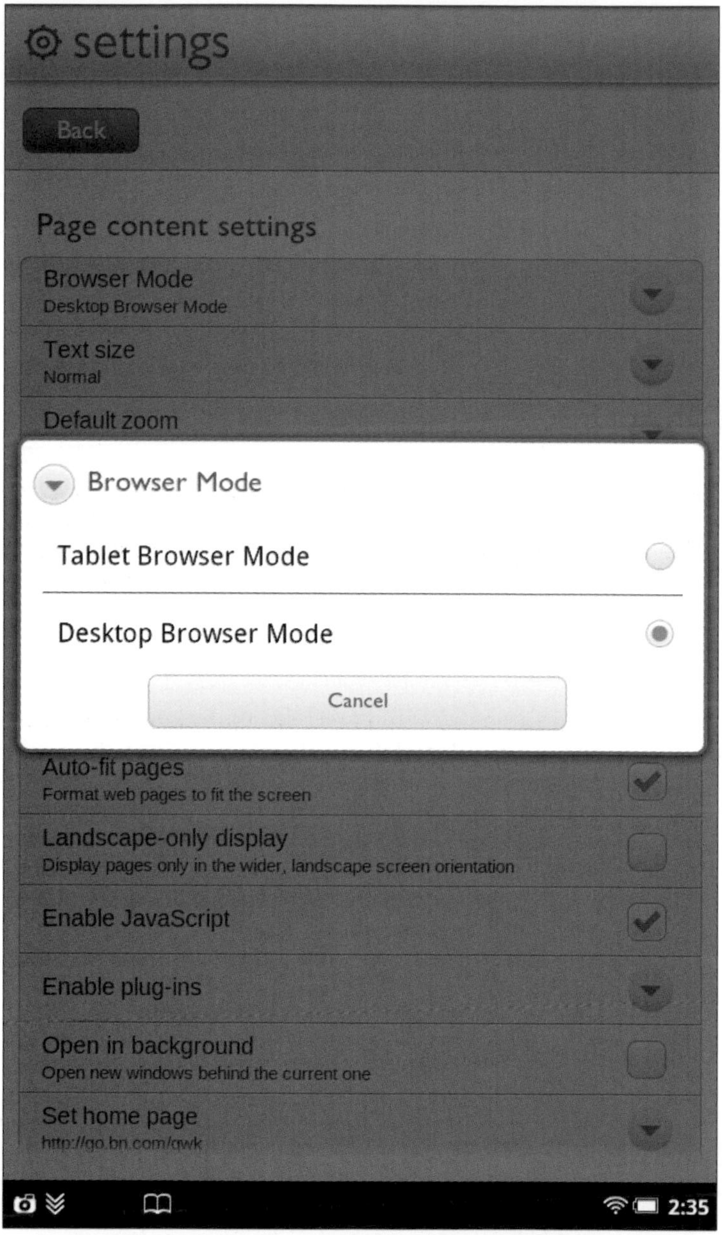

⚙ settings

Back

Page content settings

Browser Mode
Desktop Browser Mode ▼

Text size
Normal ▼

Default zoom

▼ Browser Mode

Tablet Browser Mode ○

Desktop Browser Mode ◉

Cancel

Auto-fit pages
Format web pages to fit the screen ✓

Landscape-only display
Display pages only in the wider, landscape screen orientation ☐

Enable JavaScript ✓

Enable plug-ins ▼

Open in background
Open new windows behind the current one ☐

Set home page
http://go.bn.com/qwk ▼

📷 ⌄⌄   📖   📶 🔋 2:35

Figure 7-1: You can specify the user agent for the web browser.

Improving Your NOOK Warranty

The basic warranty from Barnes & Noble protects against failure of the unit itself. If the screen stops lighting up, the speakers buzz instead of sing, or Wi-Fi is no longer wide nor well-received, the company promises to make things right: repair the device or replace it with an equivalent model (which may be new or may be a rebuilt model returned by a previous owner).

Your NOOK comes with a manufacturer warranty, and the store where you bought it may help in ways that go beyond the fine print of the guarantee. Don't be shy about calling technical support or visiting a store for help.

It's important to understand what your warranty *doesn't* cover. The warranty doesn't cover your NOOK if it takes a flying leap off your veranda, becomes caught in a folding La-Z-Boy chair, or goes splashing into the bathtub.

B&N Protection Plan

The B&N Protection Plan will replace or repair your NOOK if there's *accidental* damage two years from the day you buy it; it also handles defects. The plan isn't free. It costs about 25 percent of the original purchase price.

The plan doesn*'t* protect against these instances:

- **Purposeful mishaps:** If you admit to taking the NOOK Color into the shower, they're not going to laugh along with you.

- **Loss or theft:** To protect against that sort of occurrence, consult your insurance agent to see if you are properly protected for loss under your homeowner's or apartment renter's policy; some automobile policies also offer coverage for items that might be stolen from a car.

Extended coverage from a CC

There's another way to get a bit more coverage, and it generally comes at no extra cost. Premium-level credit cards from

American Express, MasterCard, and Visa generally offer added protection for devices that you buy using those pieces of magic plastic. For example, they might offer 90-day theft coverage from the day of purchase and a doubling of the manufacturer's warranty against failure of parts. Get in touch with customer service for any credit cards you own to see if they have this feature. Speaking for myself, I know that I always go out of my way to use this sort of card for purchases involving electronics. I've successfully collected on a claim, too.

Resetting Your NOOK

If for some reason your NOOK Color or NOOK Simple Touch just won't respond to any taps or presses, you can clear its mind by performing an electronic *reset.* Resets come in three flavors.

Resetting

A *soft reset* doesn't not erase any of the eBooks, documents, or settings. To reset, do this:

1. **Press and hold the power button for 20 seconds. Then release the power button.**

   Your NOOK will turn off.

2. **Press and hold the power button for 2 seconds to turn the NOOK back on.**

The more significant act is to perform a *hard reset,* which makes the NOOK Color exactly like it was when you got it from the factory. Barnes & Noble also calls this *erase & deregister.* Chapter 2 explains how to do this reset. Just make sure you want to erase everything from your NOOK before you do it.

Doing a total wipe (NOOK Color)

If your NOOK Color won't respond to you, and you've tried a soft reset, you can try one more extreme step: *reflash.* It returns the system folder or partition all the way back to the form and *version* that was on the device when it was first put together. (You can't do this on the NOOK Simple Touch.)

Why would you do this?

  ✔ A B&N technician told you to.

  ✔ You've tried some unofficial, warranty-violating modification of the system software and want to go back in time.

 Everything you've put on the device, including eBooks, will be gone after you follow these steps. But you can reload eBooks (at least, the ones you bought from B&N) by relinking the device to your account. You have to reinstall other eBooks and documents you side-loaded. You reinstall from a backup you made. You did make a backup first, right?

Here's how to wipe or reflash the NOOK Color:

1. **Turn the NOOK Color off by pressing and holding the power button for two seconds.**

2. **Wait a few seconds and turn it back on. Be ready...**

3. **When you see the NOOK welcome message appear on screen, press and hold the power button.**

   If you've done it right, you'll see "NOOK Color by Barnes & Noble" (either that or "Welcome to the future of reading" won't appear). The NOOK will turn off.

   On the other hand, if the animated message *does* appear, that means you *haven't* reflashed the system. In that case, start over at Step 1.

4. **On a piece of paper, write a check mark to help you keep count.**

5. **Go through the process until you've successfully interrupted the boot process *eight* times.**

   There should be eight check marks. At the eighth interruption, the NOOK Color will take over and create a fresh copy of its original operating system.

Fixing Wireless Weirdness

Fixing wireless problems sometimes feels like giving the invisible man a physical examination. You know what's supposed to be there, but you don't quite know where to poke and prod.

You have to start with a properly set up and fully working wireless network that is separate from your NOOK. The network has to be connected to a computer with a link to the Internet (or directly to a modem) at one end and be able to communicate with devices through its antenna at the other.

If you already have a Wi-Fi network, make sure it's working: Connect to it with your laptop computer or a Wi-Fi–enabled smartphone. If those devices work with the wireless network, then there's no reason your NOOK can't do the same.

If your wireless network isn't working properly, deal with that issue first. Here are some questions to ask:

- ✔ Is the Wi-Fi router on and connected to the Internet?
- ✔ Does the computer "see" and communicate with the adapter?
- ✔ Is the Internet service working? Check this from the computer.

Use your computer's troubleshooting tools. Also, each wireless device has a built-in configuration and setup screen that you can get to from your computer. Once you're sure the Wi-Fi system is working, it's time to turn your attention to your NOOK. The following sections show some potential problems and some possible solutions.

I can't find a wireless network but I know it's there

Or, you see a wireless network listed but can't keep a good connection. It may take a bit of experimentation to determine the actual working area for the Wi-Fi system you want to use.

1. **Press the ∩ button.**
2. **Tap Settings.**

3. **Tap Wireless.**

4. **Look each network's signal strength.**

    To the right of each name you'll see one to four stacked curves. Four curves means a strong signal. One curve means a weak signal, which may fade in and out.

5. **Bring the Wi-Fi router or transmitter closer to your NOOK (perhaps five or ten feet away).**

6. **Make sure no major pieces of metal block the signal.**

    That includes things like refrigerators, file cabinets, or steel desks. In some offices and homes, signals can be blocked by steel mesh used in the construction of some walls.

I see the network but my NOOK won't connect to it

Make sure you have the *key,* or password, and a user name (if they're required). The network demands that you type the key exactly and without error. If the key is 6sJ7yEllowbIRD, then that's how you must type it.

 If your Wi-Fi system is at home or the office, it might make sense to reset the Wi-Fi router to its factory default settings and reconfigure it with all of your devices ready to be connect. Read the instruction manual for the Wi-Fi system to learn how to do this.

Taking a Screenshot with the NOOK Color

The NOOK Color doesn't have a camera, but you *can* take a picture of whatever's onscreen. It's called a *screenshot.* The NOOK Simple Touch doesn't let you do this.

Here's how to grab a screenshot:

1. **Make sure the image you want is on the screen. Hold down the ⋂ button.**

2. **Briefly press the volume down button on the right edge of the device.**

   If you do it correctly (it'll probably take practice to get the timing right), you'll see a tiny camera in the status bar at the bottom of the screen. The image is saved in a folder called Screenshots found in My Files. You can view them on the NOOK with the Photo Gallery or side-load them to a computer.

Wallpapering the NOOK Color

Here's your chance to do some home (screen) decoration on the NOOK Color. Wallpaper is discussed further in Chapter 1.

Here's how to change the home screen's wallpaper:

1. **Press and hold on the existing wallpaper.**

2. **Tap Change Wallpaper. See Figure 7-2.**

3. **Tap a gallery name.**

4. **Tap the image you want to use.**

   You need a vertical image to fill the background of the Home Page.

   If you decide you do not want to change the wallpaper, tap anywhere outside the dialog box or tap Cancel.

5. **Tap Set Wallpaper.**

You can try www.NOOKColorwallpapers.com. The site, as this book went to press, was offering a wide selection of free backdrops. Free, as in no charge, no fee, no cost.

Figure 7-2: You can choose one of your own photos or use a preinstalled backdrop as wallpaper for the home page.

Going Backwards in a Hurry

There's an unpublished (except here) way to go back a screen.

To go back, swipe to the left in the small black status bar. The status bar is at the bottom of a page on the NOOK Color, and at the top of a page on the NOOK Simple Touch. The eReader will act as if you've pressed a back button. This trick doesn't work in an eBook or some other apps.

Perhaps the reason Barnes & Noble doesn't promote this gesture: If you're not *very careful* in your swiping, you can accidentally touch one of the status indicators on the bar. In that case, the swipe won't work or (even worse) it will cause perform an action you don't want. Practice makes more or less perfect.

Rooting the NOOK Color

You're about to approach the Land of Geek; it isn't a dangerous place, but it is somewhere many mere mortals choose not to tread.

Your NOOK Color and NOOK Simple Touch won't let you using apps that come from anywhere but the NOOK store. However, using a desktop or laptop computer, you can go online and search for **rooting NOOK Color**.

I don't discuss rooting your NOOK Color here because the steps often change. It's an effort by Barnes & Noble to guard its operating system and adjustments. I do discuss this topic further in the online bonus chapter for this book.

Rooting your NOOK violates the warranty that's provided by Barnes & Noble. If you have a problem with your device and B&N determines that you've rooted it, they won't honor the warranty.

However, *usually* it's possible to undo rooting and return your NOOK Color to how it was when you got it from the store. (See "Performing a Total Wipe" earlier in this chapter.)

WARNING!

Or perhaps you'd prefer to Noot

Some geeks like *Nooting* (as in NOOK rooting). Nooting changes the NOOK Color operating system to add features such as access to the Google Play Android apps and some other bells and whistles. If you take this path, you will most certainly void your NOOK warranty at least until and unless you reset it back to full factory defaults. For one path to Nooting, check out www.xda-developers.com.

If you're comfortable with working on a computer's operating system — things like changing the Windows Registry, for example — then the XDA process is something within range. If the words *Windows Registry* mean absolutely nothing to you, stay away from Nooting and consider other options.

Index